EXPERIMENTING WITH LIGHT

EXPERIMENTING WITH LIGHT

ROBERT GARDNER

FRANKLIN WATTS
CHICAGO NEW YORK LONDON TORONTO SYDNEY
A VENTURE BOOK

Illustrations by Fine Line
Photographs courtesy of: Photo Researchers Inc.: p. 15 (Alexander Lowry),
48, 49 (Berenice Abbott); Fundamental Photographs: pp. 25 (Richard Megna),
29, 38 (Peticolas/Megna), 87, 105 (Ken Kay), 115; Peter Arnold Inc.: pp. 47
(Leonard Lessin), 121; Education Development Center: pp. 84, 89, 99.

Library of Congress Cataloging-in-Publication Data

Gardner, Robert, 1929–
    Experimenting with light / Robert Gardner.
        p.   cm. — (A Venture book)
    Includes bibliographical references and index.
    Summary: Presents simple experiments that demonstrate theories of
light waves, diffraction, the effects of lenses, and reflection.
        ISBN 0-531-12520-3
    1. Light—Experiments—Juvenile literature.   [1. Light—
Experiments.   2. Experiments.]   I. Title.
QC360.G367   1991
535'.078—dc20   90-48496   CIP   AC

CONTENTS

EXPERIMENTING WITH LIGHT

INTRODUCTION

For thousands of years, human beings have found light as wonderful and awe-inspiring as they have found it useful. Most of the ancient civilizations, for example, had a sun god, and the concept of light and dark is found in many philosophies and religions.

In the Middle Ages the making of lenses, and later on the applications of lenses in telescopes and microscopes, marked the beginnings of the modern science of light and optics. In the seventeenth century, Isaac Newton formulated the laws of optics and developed a theory to explain the nature of light.

Today, scientists have a fairly good understanding of the nature and properties of light and have developed many applications, including lasers, fiber optics, and holograms. Despite our current state of knowledge, however, much remains to be learned about light, and additional applications are sure to be discovered in the future.

In this book you will carry out investigations that should lead you to an understanding of some of the fundamental properties of light. In addition, you'll learn something about the very nature of scientific inquiry and the development of scientific models.

In the first three chapters, you'll concentrate on some of the fundamental properties of light. Then, armed with a basic understanding of light gleaned from these early chapters, you'll explore a theory that explains the properties of light on the basis of waves. Finally, you'll have an opportunity to experimentally test some predictions about the behavior of light made by the wave model and examine some of the shortcomings of this model.

Many of the experiments and activities in this book were included because they are fascinating and fun to do. Most of the questions you'll encounter can be answered if you have done the experiments, analyzed the data, and thought about what you have done.

If you're somewhat familiar with the properties of light, you'll benefit most by doing those experiments that are unfamiliar to you or those that are done in a different way than you may have done them before. On the other hand, if you know relatively little about light, you may want to read the chapters and do the experiments and activities in the order they are presented. If you just want to have some fun, don't pay any attention to the questions. Just do the experiments or activities that interest you.

Regardless of your purpose in using this book, be sure to work safely. Before you begin, read the following safety rules.

SAFETY FIRST

1. Do any experiments, whether from this book or of your own design, under the supervision of a qualified science teacher or other knowledgeable adult.

2. Read all instructions carefully before proceeding with a project. If you have questions, check with your supervisor before going any further.

3. Maintain a serious attitude while conducting experiments. Fooling around can be dangerous to you and to others.

4. Wear approved safety goggles when you are experimenting or are in a laboratory setting.

5. Do not eat or drink while experimenting.

6. Have safety equipment such as fire extinguishers, fire blankets, and first-aid kits nearby while you are experimenting. Know where this equipment is and how to use it properly.

7. Do not touch any high-voltage source or anything connected to a high-voltage source.

8. Never experiment with household electricity except under the supervision of a knowledgeable adult.

9. Light bulbs produce light, but they also produce heat. Don't touch a lit high-wattage bulb.

10. Never look directly at the sun. It can cause permanent damage to your eyes.

1
REFLECTION

Everyone seems to assume that light travels in straight lines. When a hunter sights down a gun barrel, or when a carpenter looks along the edge of a board, or when a surveyor looks through a transit or a photographer through a viewfinder, or when a driver looks into a rear-view mirror, all operate under the assumption that light travels in straight lines. Their success in bagging a bird, building a house, mapping land, taking a fine picture, or preventing an accident is confirmation that their assumption is correct, at least for the accuracy required for their purposes.

Other observations confirm the straight-line motion of light. If you look through a long, narrow, straight tube, you will see only the objects directly in front of your eye. The edges of shadows cast by light from the sun or a light bulb are straight, as you can see in the photograph on page 15. A ship's pilot cannot see the light from a lighthouse beyond a certain distance even in very clear air: the earth curves, but light doesn't. You'll see additional evidence for the straight-line motion of light, and some exceptions to the rule, as you experiment with light and waves.

REFLECTION: A SIMPLE EXPERIMENT • With a sheet of paper, a pencil, a little clay, and a microscope slide, you can investigate the basic law of reflection. Just follow the steps listed below using Figure 1 as a guide. If you don't have a microscope slide, you can substitute a small pane of glass (**tape all but one of its long edges to prevent being cut**), or one side of a clear plastic box.

Step 1. Use the slide, or its substitute, to draw a straight line on a sheet of paper. Label the line *LN*.

Step 2. Draw another line *IR* at an angle to *LN*. This line represents a ray of light that travels to the glass. A ray of light is a very thin beam of light. Ideally, it has no dimensions, but in this book we will simply use as narrow a beam as possible to represent a ray.

Step 3. Hold the edge of the front surface of the slide on the line *LN*. If necessary, use a small piece of clay to hold the slide upright.

Step 4. Look into the slide. In reasonably bright light you can see the reflected image of the line *IR* through the slide. Use a pencil to make two dots in front

**The edges of shadows cast by light
from the sun are straight.**

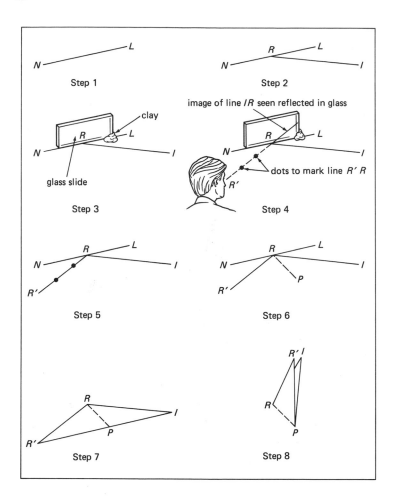

Figure 1. Investigating the law of reflection.

of the slide along an imaginary line *RR'*. This imaginary line *RR'* should be along the extension of the image of the line *IR* that you see reflected in the slide. The extension goes from the slide to your eye.

Step 5. Use the slide or another straight edge to draw the line *RR'* connecting the dots. Extend the line to meet *LN*, which marks the reflecting surface of the slide. This new line *RR'* represents the reflection of a light ray that traveled to the glass slide along the line *IR*. The light traveling along *RR'* is called the *reflected ray*. It comes *from* the slide. The light that came *to* the glass along the line *IR* is called the *incident ray*.

Step 6. Use a corner of the slide or its substitute to draw a line *PR* perpendicular to *LN* at the point where *IR* and *RR'* meet. In geometry and physics, a line perpendicular to another line is often called a *normal*.

Step 7. Cut the paper along the lines *IR* and *RR'*. Remove this triangular piece of paper from the rest of the sheet.

Step 8. Fold the triangle along *PR*, the line perpendicular to *LN*. The line *LN*, you'll remember, marks the reflecting surface of the slide.

How does the angle between *IR* and *PR*, the *angle of incidence*, compare with the angle between *RR'* and *PR*, *the angle of reflection*? What does this tell you about the way light is reflected? Do you think the same relationship will hold true for other angles of incidence? How can you find out?

If you looked carefully when you drew *RR'* along the extended image of *IR*, you probably saw two images of *IR*, one brighter than the other. How do you explain these two images? Why do you think one is brighter than the other? Which image did you use in drawing *RR'*? Do you think you chose the right one?

You can repeat this experiment using a plane mirror in place of the glass slide and common pins instead of the line *IR* to define the rays. Draw a line on a piece of paper that rests on a sheet of soft cardboard. Place the reflecting surface of a mirror on the line. Support the mirror upright with a small piece of clay. Use a pair of common pins to define an incident ray to the mirror as shown in Figure 2. Pins 3 and 4, which are used to define the reflected ray, can be lined up with the *images* of pins 1 and 2. Pins 3 and 4 on the reflected ray will be along a line that extends through the images of *both* the pins that define the incident ray as seen in the mirror.

Use a pencil and straight edge to draw the incident and reflected rays going to and coming from the mirror as defined by the pins. Now draw a line perpendicular to the line marking the mirror's reflecting surface at the point where the incident and reflected rays meet. How does the angle between the normal and the incident ray (the angle of incidence) compare with the angle between the reflected ray and the normal (the angle of reflection)?

Repeat the experiment using different angles of incidence. What can you conclude about the angle of incidence and the angle of reflection?

WHERE IS YOUR MIRROR IMAGE? • When you look into a mirror, your image may appear to you to be behind the mirror. But how can that be, especially when the mirror is mounted on a solid wall as many mirrors are? Perhaps the image is on the mirror or in front of the mirror. In this experiment, you'll find out where your image really is.

To locate an image seen in a plane mirror, first draw a straight line on a sheet of paper. Place the paper on a sheet of soft cardboard. Then use a piece of clay or a

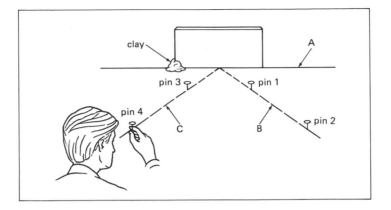

Figure 2. Measuring the angles that light rays make with a mirror. A—Line to mark reflecting surface of mirror. B—Incident ray defined by pins 1 and 2. C—Reflected ray defined by pins 3 and 4.

block and a rubber band to support a mirror upright on the paper. Be sure that the silvered side of the mirror is on the line you drew. Stick a large pin or a nail that is taller than the mirror about 10 to 15 centimeters (cm) in front of the mirror. Use a pair of common pins to make a sight line to the *image* of the large pin or nail that you can see in the mirror. See Figure 3. Make a number of sight lines from different places. Use a pair of common pins for each one. All these sight lines should meet at the location of the image.

Remove the mirror and use a straight edge to draw the sight lines. Where was the image? Was it on the mirror? Behind the mirror? In front of the mirror? How

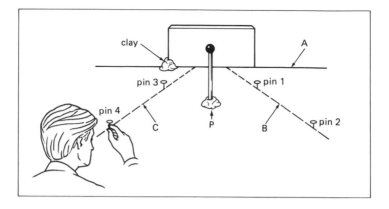

Figure 3. Locating a mirror image. A—One sight line to the image. B—Another sight line to the image. C—A line marking the reflecting surface of the mirror. P—A large pin or nail whose image in the mirror is to be located.

does the distance from the pin or nail to the mirror compare with the distance from its image to the mirror?

Place the pin or nail to one side of the mirror instead of directly in front of it. Where is the image now? How does the perpendicular distance from the pin or nail to the plane of the mirror compare with the perpendicular distance from the image to the plane of the mirror?

Look at two objects that are almost along the same sight line but at different distances from you. When you move your head, or close first one eye and then the other, the two objects will appear to shift relative to one another. We say they show *parallax*. However, if two objects are at the same place, they do not shift relative to one another when you change your position. There is no parallax between them. We can use the absence of parallax to locate images seen in a mirror.

Put a tall stick at the point where the image of the pin or nail was located according to the sight lines you drew. Replace the mirror and look into it. You should be able to see the top of the stick at the image position sticking up above the mirror. It should line up with the bottom of the pin's image as seen in the mirror. Furthermore, if the stick is at the location of the image, the image of the pin and the top of the stick should stay together when you move your head or close first one eye and then the other.

Use the lack of parallax to locate the image when the object is at various positions in front of and to the side of the mirror. What do you conclude about the positions of object and image?

A CLOSE LOOK AT YOUR IMAGE • You may have heard people say, "It's turned around like a mirror image" or "It's reversed like a mirror image." Pause a moment and look closely at your image in a mirror. Is it reversed? Is it upside down? On which side of the image, as you look at it, is your left shoulder? Your right ear? What is it about your image that's really different from you?

Try to read a message you've printed while holding it in front of a mirror. Can you write the message so that it can be read easily in the mirror?

VIRTUAL IMAGES IN A PLANE MIRROR • You've learned that the image of an object seen in a plane mirror is located behind the mirror. Furthermore, the distance from the plane of the mirror to the image is equal to the distance from the mirror to the object in the opposite direction.

But how could your image be located in a wall? Obviously, it couldn't really be there, but it certainly *appears* to be there. That's why the images seen in plane mirrors are called *virtual* images; they only *appear* to be behind the mirror. That's where the reflected rays that we use to see the images indicate them to be. You can't find virtual images by looking behind the mirror.

To see how a pair of light rays coming from an object actually behave, cut a pair of narrow slits in a piece of black construction paper. Refer to Figure 4. The slits should be about 1 millimeter (mm) wide, 3 cm high, and 2 cm apart. Fold the paper so it will stand upright and the slits will be vertical. Then, in an otherwise dark room, let the light from a nearby light bulb shine through the slits. This will provide you with two narrow, diverging (spreading-apart) beams of light that represent two incident rays I_1 and I_2. Reflect the light beams with a mirror and you'll see that if you were to look at only the reflected light, it would appear to be coming from a point behind the mirror.

Using the law of reflection (the angle of incidence equals the angle of reflection) and a little geometry, see whether you can show that the image of an object is as far behind the mirror as the object is in front. Start with a single point of light. Once you've shown it to be true for a point of light, you can show it to be true for both ends of an object and then the entire object.

Can you show that the virtual image formed by a plane mirror will have the same size as the object?

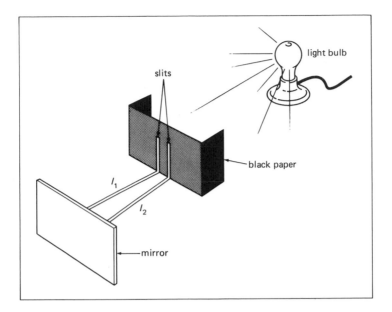

Figure 4. Light rays being reflected by a mirror.

The fact that virtual images are symmetrical with the objects that give rise to them can lead to some "science magic." One example is shown in Figure 5. The image of a candle burning in front of a pane of glass in a dark room appears to be a real candle burning under water. A jar of water is placed at the position of the candle's virtual image, and the actual candle is screened from viewers' eyes. With a little imagination you can probably design some similar "science magic."

MIRRORS AT AN ANGLE ● If you look in a mirror, you see an image. But suppose you place two mirrors next to each other at an angle. Will you see more than one

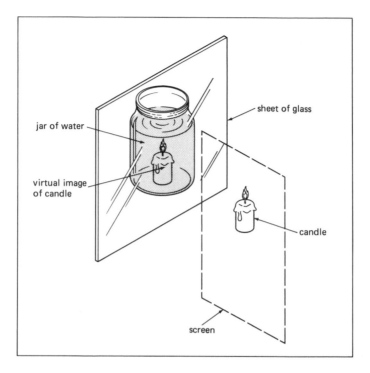

**Figure 5. Making a candle appear
to burn underwater.**

image, as is shown in the photograph on page 25? Does
the number you see depend on the angle between the
mirrors (Figure 6)?

To find out, obtain two mirrors as nearly identical
as possible. On a sheet of white paper, draw lines at
angles of 180°, 120°, 90°, 60°, 45°, 30°, and 15° from
some given lines. Begin by placing the *reflecting surfaces* of the two mirrors on the 180° lines. Clay or
wooden blocks can be used to support the mirrors if
necessary. Place a pencil or a pin, supported by a lump

How many mirrors and cars do you think were present when this photograph was taken?

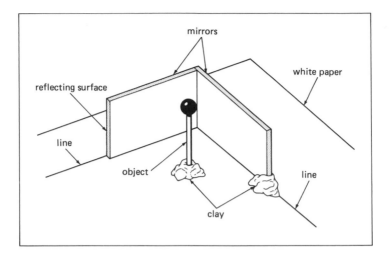

**Figure 6. Experimenting with
mirrors at an angle.**

of clay, in front of the mirrors. You'll not be surprised to
see but one image of the object in the mirrors. All you've
done, after all, is to turn two mirrors into one. You
probably won't be surprised to see two images in the two
mirrors at an angle of 120° either, but look what happens
when the mirrors are at right angles! How many images
of the object can you see now?

If possible, put your face very close to the mirrors
and look at your own images. Look closely at the middle image and wink your right eye. Which eye does the
image appear to wink? How do you think this middle
image is formed?

How many images of the object do you see when
the mirrors are at angles of 60°? 45°? 30°? 15°? To see
whether there is any relationship between the angle and

the number of images, plot a graph of the number of images as a function of the angle between the mirrors. Since the angle is the *independent variable*, the variable that you manipulate in the experiment, it should be plotted on the horizontal axis according to convention. The number of images you see depends on the angle between the mirrors, so it is called the *dependent variable*. It should be plotted on the vertical axis.

What does the graph tell you? See whether you an use the graph to predict the angle that will give four images. Then try it. Does it work?

Can you use your graph to predict the number of images you will see when the mirrors are parallel, that is, when the angle between the mirrors is 0°? Arrange two mirrors so their reflecting surfaces are parallel and about 30 cm apart. Place an object between them. How many images are there? You might enjoy standing between two such mirrors hung on opposite walls of a hallway. How many images of you do you see? Can you explain why?

2
BENDING LIGHT: REFRACTION AND COLOR

The photograph on page 29 shows a beam of light striking a glass block. As you can see, some light in the beam is reflected, but some of the light passes through the glass and emerges from the other side. Notice how the light bends sharply when it enters and leaves the glass. You can see the same effect if you put a pencil in a glass of water and look at it from the side. The "broken pencil effect" is the result of light bending as it goes from water to air. This bending of light as it passes from one transparent medium, such as air, into another, such as glass or water, is called *refraction*. It's

Light from source *S* striking the block of glass in this photograph is both reflected (beams marked *A*) and refracted (beams marked *B*).

one of the exceptions to the rule that light travels in straight lines.

The paths followed by light that moves through lenses, along light "pipes," and through prisms can be predicted from the laws of reflection and refraction. In this chapter you'll have an opportunity to explore the refraction of light and perhaps come to an understanding that will enable you to predict the paths that light will take in different transparent materials.

You'll find, too, that refraction can change white light into a rainbow of colored lights. You probably know that if you mix blue and yellow paints you will get green. A red sweater is seen as red because when white light shines on it, it reflects red light and absorbs the other colors in white light. Such a process is characteristic of pigments. The formation of colors in this way is called the *subtractive* method of color mixing because each pigment removes (subtracts) colors from white light.

What happens if you mix colors by adding different colored lights together on a screen instead of absorbing the colors with pigments? The results of this *additive* method of color mixing, as you will see, are quite different from those obtained by the subtractive method.

MEASURING REFRACTION • To see how light is refracted by water, you can use a pair of pins to define a "ray" of light. Let the ray enter a plastic box filled with water as shown in Figure 7a. Be sure to mark the sides of the box with a pencil as shown in the drawing. If you should accidentally move the box, the lines will allow you to put it back in the same place. With another pair of

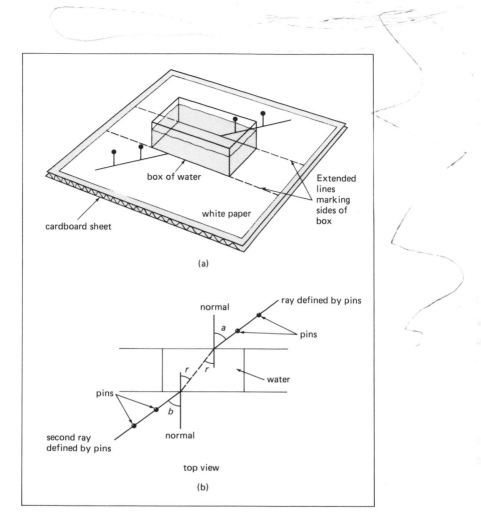

label: box of water
label: white paper
label: Extended lines marking sides of box
label: cardboard sheet

(a)

normal
a
ray defined by pins
pins
r *r*
water
pins
b
second ray defined by pins
normal

top view

(b)

Figure 7. A light ray passing from air to water to air.

pins you can find the path of the light ray after it has passed through the water. Simply line them up with the first two pins, which you can see by looking *through* the water. Since light travels in straight lines through any

31

one medium, the path of the light through the water must be along the dotted line shown in Figure 7b.

Do the pins line up if you look at them through the other side of the box? Is the path of refracted light rays the same when they travel in the opposite direction?

Use the pins, a pencil, and a ruler to draw lines to mark the rays to and from the box as well as the path the light follows through the water. Measure angle *a*, the angle between the ray going to the box, and a line perpendicular to the box at the point where the light enters the water. (This perpendicular line, called the *normal*, is shown in Figure 7b.) Measure angle *b* on the other side of the box as shown in the drawing.

You have probably found that angles *a* and *b* are equal, or very nearly so. What does this tell you about the rays of light going to and coming from the box?

If you know basic trigonometry, you can go on with this experiment. If not, you may want to move on to the section Twinkling Light.

Measure angle *r*, the angle between the normal and the light ray within the water. It's called, quite logically, the angle of refraction. How does it compare with the angles of incidence (*a* and *b*)? If you were to measure a large number of incident angles and their corresponding angles of refraction for light passing from air to water, your data table would look like the one in Table 1.

It looks as if there may be a relationship between the angles of incidence and refraction. Is the ratio of angle *i* to angle *r* constant? To find out, plot a graph using the data in Table 1. Plot the angles of incidence, *i* on the vertical axis and their corresponding angles of

Table 1		Table 2	
Angle of incidence (i)	Angle of refraction (r)	Sine of angle of incidence ($\sin i$)	Sine of angle of refraction ($\sin r$)
10°	7.5°	0.174	0.131
20°	14.9°	0.342	0.257
30°	22.0°	0.500	0.375
40°	28.8°	0.643	0.482
50°	35.1°	0.766	0.575
60°	40.6°	0.866	0.651
70°	45.0°	0.940	0.707
80°	48.8°	0.985	0.752

refraction, r, on the horizontal axis. The graph looks straight for the first few points, but then what happens?

For any right triangle, the sine of an acute angle is the ratio of the side opposite the angle to the hypotenuse. The values for the sines of the angles in Table 1 are given in Table 2. Use them to plot a graph of the sine of the angle of incidence as a function of the sine of the corresponding angle of refraction. What do you find? What is the slope (rise/run) of your graph?

THE INDEX OF REFRACTION • The ratio of the sine of the angle of incidence to the sine of the angle of refraction ($\sin i / \sin r$) when light passes from air into a substance is called the *index of refraction* of that substance. It is a characteristic property of substances that transmit light.

For water, the index is 1.33, as you can find from the slope of the graph of sin *i* vs. sin *r*.

Using the same apparatus that you used to measure the angles of incidence and refraction for water, find the index of refraction of antifreeze. For accuracy, choose an angle of incidence of about 45°. You can also use the apparatus to find the index of refraction of rubbing alcohol, glycerine, and a concentrated solution of salt and water. How do the indices of refraction of these liquids compare?

With some care, you can investigate the effect of the concentration of a sugar solution on its index of refraction. As you make the solution more and more concentrated, what happens to its index of refraction? Is there a relationship between the concentration and the index of refraction for sugar?

Design an experiment to measure the index of refraction of a solid such as glass or plastic. What do you find?

TWINKLING LIGHT • You've probably heard the children's poem that begins "Twinkle, twinkle little star . . . ," and you may have seen just such a star twinkling in the night sky. Twinkling stars are often seen near the horizon because their light passes through more atmosphere than does light from stars nearer the zenith. As the earth cools, air currents are set up as cold air sinks and warm air rises. Since the index of refraction of air is related to its temperature, light bends as it passes through air masses of different temperature. The result is a shifting of the light's path as it travels through the atmosphere. You've probably seen a similar effect in the summer when you look at objects through the air above the hot pavement of a highway.

You can use a laser to simulate this twinkling effect if one is available. **Ask a teacher or another adult to help you shine the beam from a low-power laser** (1 milliwatt) over a hot plate or one of the heating elements of an electric stove. **Be sure you don't touch the hot plate, and don't look directly into the laser!** Instead, watch the light "twinkle" on a screen where it can be safely reflected to your eyes.

If you don't have access to a laser, place a piece of cardboard with a pinhole through it in front of the beam of an empty slide projector. Move a magnifying glass between the pinhole and a screen or light-colored wall until you have as small a patch of light as possible on the screen or wall. Fasten the magnifying glass in this position with tape and/or a holder so that the small patch of light remains fixed and steady. Then put a hot plate just below the light beam so that the light must pass through turbulent air before reaching the screen. Stand back and watch your twinkling "star" on the screen.

A "MAGIC" LENS • You may be able to convince your friends that you have a magic lens or that different-colored letters are affected in different ways by a cylindrical lens. Before you do, try this little investigation. Write your name in capital letters on a piece of paper. Then fill a plastic vial, an olive or spice jar, or a test tube with water and seal it. (A clear vial such as the kind in which pills are sold will do.) Place the water-filled cylinder in a horizontal position on the print. You may have to raise the tube slightly to see the images clearly. At the right height above the print, you will see your name with the letters upside down. Why?

Now write the words HI-DE-HO TO YOU along a line on a piece of paper. Write HI-DE-HO in blue ink. Write TO YOU in red ink. Again, place the cylindrical lens on the letters as shown in Figure 8. If necessary, raise the lens and support it in some way so that the letters in TO YOU are clearly inverted. HI-DE-HO will appear unchanged. Perhaps you can convince people that the color of the letters affects the way light is bent by the lens. In any event, let them ponder the problem until someone tries writing the letters H, I, D, E, and O upside down. Can you explain what you see in the photograph on page 37?

TOTAL INTERNAL REFLECTION • Sometimes refracted light that enters one side of a transparent material does

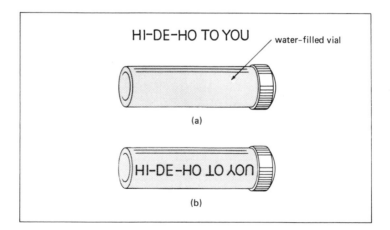

Figure 8. A view through a "magic" lens (a) before it is placed on the letters and (b) after it is placed on the letters.

**Can you figure out
how the upside-down
image was created?**

not come out the other side. Instead, *all* the light is reflected at the second surface. This is called *total internal reflection*. Whether the light is totally reflected depends on the angle at which the light strikes the internal surface and on the nature of the material in which the light is moving. The minimum angle of incidence at which this happens is called the *critical angle*.

It's quite easy to show total internal reflection in glass. All you need is a right-angle prism and a narrow beam of light. You can make the narrow beam of light with a slit as before (see Figure 4), but this time make only one slit in the paper. Position the light source 2–3 meters (m) from the slit. If you let the narrow beam of light strike the longest flat surface of a 45-45-90 prism at an angle of incidence of 0°, it will be incident on a second side of the prism at 45°. For all angles greater than 42° (the critical angle for glass), all the light will be reflected to the third side, where the angle of incidence will be 45° too. As a result, the light beam will emerge from the prism at 180° from its point of entry, as shown in Figure 9.

Why do you think the light that emerges from the prism is dimmer than the light that entered? What use might be made of right-angle prisms in optical instruments? See whether you can build a periscope using right-angle prisms. Then build one using mirrors. Which do you prefer? How are commercial periscopes made?

DISPERSION • If you look at light that passes through glass at angles close to but slightly less than 42°, you'll see the light break up into the colors of the rainbow as it enters air. This pattern of colored light is called a *spec-*

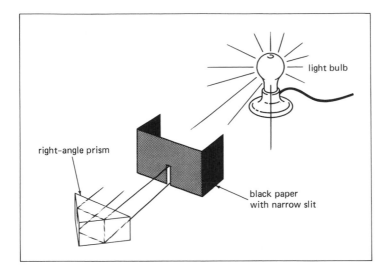

Figure 9. Total internal reflection in a 45-45-90 prism.

trum. To see the effect, hold an ordinary glass or plastic prism in sunlight, but **don't look directly at the sun.** If you turn the prism in certain ways, you'll be able to see a spectrum formed by light that passes through the prism.

To examine the spectrum more closely, make a narrow beam of light as you did before with the light about 1 m from the slit. Put a glass or plastic prism on the beam, as shown in Figure 10. Set up a screen to prevent bright light from falling on the spectrum. You can see that not all light is refracted in the same way. The separation of light into colors by refraction is called *dispersion*. Which visible color is refracted most? Which is refracted least? How does the index of refraction of blue light compare with the index for red light?

39

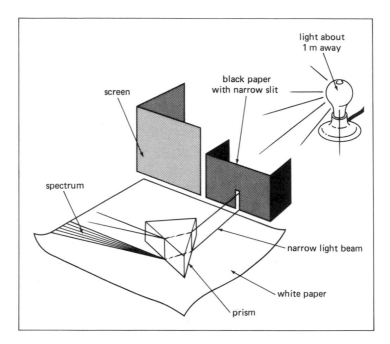

Figure 10. A spectrum produced by refracting white light.

Try using the corner of a water-filled plastic box. Can you obtain a spectrum using water instead of the prism?

USING A PRISM TO MIX COLORED LIGHT • You can produce a brilliant spectrum in a dark room using a prism and a narrow beam of light from a slide projector (Figure 11). Remove the film from an old slide and replace it with a small square of thin cardboard in which you have carefully cut a narrow slit about 1 mm wide and 3 cm long. Tape this piece of cardboard to the old

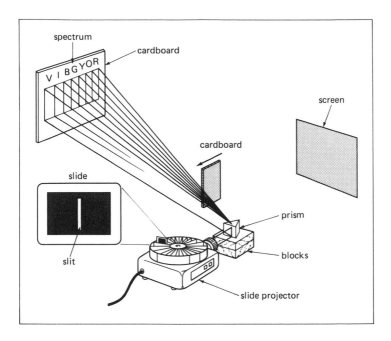

Figure 11. Using a slide projector, prism, and screen to mix colored light.

slide and put it in the projector with the slit in a vertical position. Focus the image of the slit on a screen several meters in front of the projector. Then stand the prism upright on some blocks so that it intercepts the line of light emerging from the projector. Adjust the prism carefully until it bends the light to form a beautiful sharp spectrum some distance to the right or left of the screen. "Capture" this spectrum on a flat white surface such as a large sheet of white cardboard, a white board, a piece of Styrofoam, or some other flat, white surface.

Now look at the spectrum from *grazing angle*, that is, with your line of sight almost parallel to the surface of the screen—at 90° to the colored light beam coming to the screen. The fine line of light that you see now appears to be white. With all the colors entering your eye together, the mixture is seen as white. To convince yourself that you really are seeing a mixture of colors, have a partner place a piece of cardboard in the beam so that only red light gets to the screen. Now when you look at the spectrum at grazing angle you'll see red light. If only blue light reaches the screen, you'll see blue light. With two pieces of cardboard, your partner can remove both the blue and red ends of the spectrum so you can view the light coming from the middle of the spectrum. What color do you see?

Have your partner block out the red end of the spectrum but leave all the violet, blue, and green. The color you see when you view this mixture of blue and green at grazing angle is called *cyan*. What color do you see when you mix green and red?

To obtain a mixture of the red and blue ends of the spectrum, have your partner place the screen in the colored light beam and turn it so it is at a sharp angle (almost parallel) to the beam. By adjusting the angle carefully, he or she can block out the central green region of the spectrum so that only the light from the blue and red ends of the spectrum reaches the screen. The mixture of blue and red light that you see at grazing angle is called *magenta*.

At large distances from the slide projector, the spectrum will be quite large. You can place small colored objects in different parts of the spectrum and see how they appear to change color. For example, what is the color of a red object in the green region of the spectrum? In the blue region? In the red region? How about a yellow object in the red region? In the green region? In blue light? After a few trials, perhaps you'll be able to predict the color that a certain colored object will have in each colored area of the spectrum.

PROJECTING AND MIXING COLORED LIGHTS • A better but more expensive way to mix colored lights is to use three overhead projectors or slide projectors. These projectors have large lenses that refract and focus light on a screen or white wall. If your school has three such projectors, you may be able to borrow them for this investigation. If only one such projector is available, you can still mix colors, but all three colors will have to be produced on or in the same projector. For example, you can punch three holes in a small piece of a file folder or some other thin cardboard made to fit a slide. Tape red, blue, and green filters over these holes. The colored light beams coming from the projector can then be mixed by using mirrors to reflect the beams onto the same area of a screen.

For overhead projectors, cut three sheets of cardboard that will completely cover each of the flat surfaces where people normally write on the projector. Cut a circle about 10–12 cm in diameter in the center of each sheet. Cover the opening in one sheet with a piece of red plastic that filters out all the colors except red. Cover another with a sheet of green plastic and the third with a blue filter. Good filters can be obtained from a company that supplies light filters (gels) for theaters or from one of the science supply houses found in the appendix. If you use three slide projectors, cut holes in three heavy paper or light cardboard slides and cover them with red, green, and blue filters.

If these colored light beams from either type of projectors are focused onto a screen, you can mix any combination you want. You know that the combination of all three colors should give white, so you might begin by letting all three colors overlap. Then move the projectors closer or farther from the screen until the region where all three beams overlap is white. What color do you find when red and blue are mixed by the additive method? How about red and green? Blue and green?

In addition to mixing colors, you also might like to examine the colored shadows that can be produced with these colored light beams. Two beams will produce two shadows, of course. But what color will the shadows be in the areas where the beams overlap if the two beams are red and blue? Red and green? Blue and green? Can you predict the colors of the three shadows produced if all three colored beams are used?

Now that you think you know all about color mixing and colored shadows, try this: Remove the colored filter that covers one of the holes from which the colored beams come so that it will provide a beam of white light. Look carefully at the two shadows produced when this white beam is coupled with a red beam. One shadow is red. That's not surprising, but look closely at the other shadow. It has a light cyan color. Can you explain why? Can you predict the colors of the shadows you'll get with white and green beams? With white and blue beams?

You can also use these colored beams to see what

colored objects look like in different-colored light as was suggested using the spectrum formed by a prism. After a few trials, perhaps you'll be able to predict the color that a certain colored object will have in each colored area on the screen. If not, you can have fun trying.

3
PINHOLES AND STROBOSCOPES

Photography is a wonderful medium that allows people to capture the images of objects on film. Although modern cameras are complex instruments, photographs also can be taken using very simple cameras. For example, the right-hand half of the photograph on page 47 was taken using a pinhole camera, a device essentially consisting of little more than film and a box containing a pinhole. Of course, most photographers don't work this way, and many tend to use fancy cameras with lots of accessories. The photograph at the top of pages 48 and 49, for example, was taken using a

The right-hand photograph was taken using a
pinhole camera, while the left-hand
photograph of the same scene was taken using
a standard 35-mm camera. Although there is
a distinct difference in quality, the
pinhole photograph is remarkably clear.
Some famous photographers, including
Ansel Adams, have experimented with pinhole
cameras in their search for different
means of capturing an image.

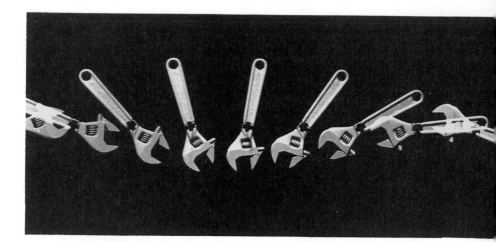

A moving wrench photographed using a strobe light. The horizontal movement of the dark crosses at the top of the handle indicates that the wrench is turning about its center of mass.

strobe, a device that enables the user to "stop" a moving object in time. In this chapter, you will learn about pinholes and strobes.

PINHOLES AND CAMERA OBSCURAS • Long before cameras were invented, a number of artists had discovered a way to produce real images on a screen or canvas. These artists worked in a dark room called a *camera obscura*, where the only light entering the room came through a small hole. Light coming from the natural scene the artist wished to paint passed through the hole, producing an upside-down image of the view outside. Once the colorful slice of nature had been "captured" on

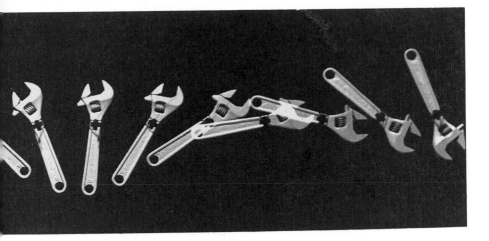

a canvas, the artist proceeded to fill in the image with paints that matched the natural colors transmitted from outside. Are camera obscuras the forerunners of pinhole cameras?

Pinholes in one form or another have a number of practical applications. Have you ever noticed how much more clearly you can see something if you look at it through a pinhole or a narrow tube made by rolling up a piece of paper? You may be surprised to find that a pinhole can be used to magnify print. Could this perhaps explain why people squint when they have difficulty seeing something?

Pinhole images can be observed on an almost daily basis. You'll see them created when sunlight passes through narrow openings around shades or curtains. On a bright summer's day, notice the hundreds of round images of the sun that can be seen on the ground in the shade of a tree. What do you suppose makes these sun dapples, as they are called?

PINHOLE OPTICS • Use a pin or needle to make a pinhole, about 1 mm in diameter, in a file card. Then move your eye close to some small print in a magazine or newspaper until the print becomes blurry, that is, until the lens of your eye is no longer able to bend the light enough to focus it on your retina. With your eye in this position, bring the pinhole close to your eye. You'll find that you can now see the print quite clearly. If you slowly move the pinhole away from your eye toward the page, the print will appear larger as it would with a magnifying glass.

To further investigate the images produced by pinholes you'll need to work in a dark room and use a clear (unfrosted) light bulb (preferably one with a straight-line filament) and socket. Refer to Figure 12 for the following directions.

Cut away the flaps that make up the top of a box that is about 30 cm on each side. Also, cut a few holes in the top of the box to allow heat to escape. Tape a piece of black construction paper over a square hole cut in one side of the box. The center of the hole should be at the same height as the bulb's filament. Place the bulb so the socket is just inside the open end of the box. **Be sure the bulb does not touch the box because heat from the bulb could ignite the cardboard.** Then make a tiny pinhole through the center of the black paper. Place a screen beyond the pinhole and darken the room.

Now turn on the light. The image you see on the screen is called a *pinhole image*. To see why, cover the pinhole. What happens to the image?

Move the screen closer to the pinhole. What happens to the size of the image? What happens to the size

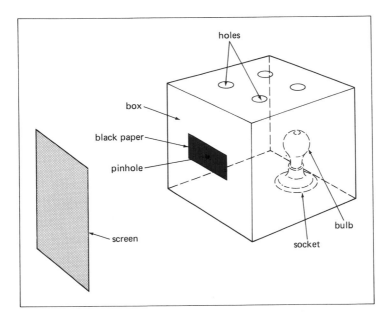

Figure 12. Making pinhole images.

of the image as you move the screen farther from the pinhole?

In Figure 13, you can see how light rays from the object pass through a pinhole to form an image. On the basis of the drawing, should the image be right side up or upside down? Should it be turned right for left? Slowly move the tip of a pencil up and down in front of the bulb. Then move it in front of the bulb from the right or left. Where does the shadow of the pencil first appear on the image? Were your predictions correct? Why do you think the pinhole image of the filament is so much dimmer than the bright filament itself?

Look again at Figure 13. Triangle *PTB* is similar to triangle *PT'B'*. Why? If you place the screen the same distance from the pinhole as the filament, how will the size of the image compare with the size of the filament? Try it! Were you right? How will image size compare with object (filament) size if the screen is *twice* as far from the pinhole as the filament? If the screen is *half* as far from the pinhole as the object?

What do you think you'll find if you punch a second pinhole in the black paper close to the first one? A third hole? Suppose you make a bigger pinhole; how will that affect the clarity and brightness of the image? Test your predictions.

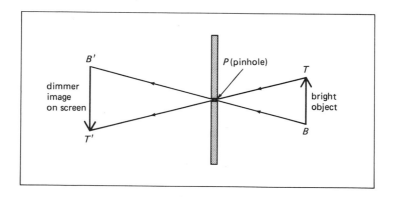

Figure 13. The formation of a pinhole image.

A PINHOLE PUZZLER • Now that you're an expert on pinhole images, here are a couple of pinhole experiments to ponder. You'll need an opaque plastic 35-mm film container and a common pin. Use a large pin or needle to make a pinhole about 1 mm in diameter near the center of the bottom of the container (Figure 14a). Use a common pin to make a hole through the side of the container about 0.5 cm from the open (top) end of the container. Put the *head* of the common pin inside the container and push the sharp end out through the hole you made in the side. **To prevent getting cut, wrap a piece of tape around the sharp end of the pin that now sticks out from the side of the container** (Figure 14b).

Hold the pinhole end of the container close to your eye (Figure 14c). Turn the pinhole toward a well-illuminated wall, grasp the taped end of the pin, and slowly move the head of the pin up and down inside the container. Notice that if the pinhead is oriented downward, you can see its dark shadow oriented downward; if it is turned upward, you can see its shadow with an upward orientation. In other words, you see the pin as it is. Now turn the container around so that you hold the open end close to your eye (Figure 14d). Again, move the head of the pin up and down. This time the pin's shadow appears to be upside down. Why should the pin's shadow appear right side up in one case and upside down in the other?

If the light is bright enough, you may notice that the edge of the shadow has a bluish tint while the edge of the circle of light is yellowish. If not, use a light bulb as the light source to see this color effect. **Do not use the sun!** Can you think of a way to explain this effect? (Remember what you learned in Chapter 2 about disper-

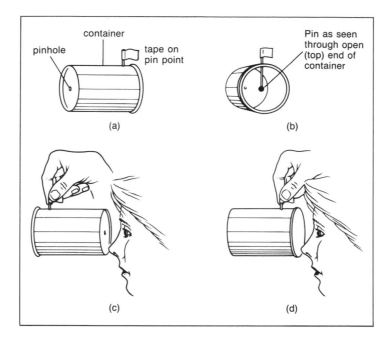

**Figure 14. Setting up
pinhole puzzlers.**

sion and the differences in the refractive index of colored light.)

Remove the pin from the container. **Without the
pin,** you can prove to yourself that the dark shadow
around the circle of light is the shadow cast by the iris,
the colored part of your eye. Close both eyes for several
minutes so that they become partially adapted to darkness. This will cause the iris diaphragms to open wider

as they normally do in dim light. Hold the open end of the **pinless** container against one open eye, keeping the other eye closed. Look at the bright wall. Now open the other eye; you'll see the bright circle shrink. The iris diaphragms of both eyes respond to bright light entering either one. To see that this is true, stand in front of a mirror and open your eyes wide so that you can see the pupils clearly. (The pupils are the holes in the irises.) Cover one eye and watch the pupil of your open eye enlarge as the iris responds in reflex fashion to the reduced light. When you uncover your eye, you'll see the pupil shrink in the eye you've been watching.

Look through the open end of the **pinless** container once more. This time concentrate on the circle of light. You'll see a number of little circles of light with dark circles around them that seem to drift slowly about in the field of view. These are the shadows cast by tiny particles in the fluid inside your eyeball. You'll understand why there are bright and dark circles in the shadows after you've investigated diffraction in Chapter 5.

A PINHOLE CAMERA • Use flat black paint to blacken the walls of a small, light-tight box about the size of a shoe box. Cut a small square hole in the center of the front end of the box so that a piece of black cardboard with a pinhole through it can be taped over the opening. Before you add film to the "camera," cover the pinhole with a small piece of black tape. Cut a flap in the back of the box so that a piece of film can be taped to it in a photographer's darkroom or a very dark closet.

Once your camera has been loaded with film, place it on a stable support, turn it toward the subject you wish to photograph, and open the pinhole. You'll have to learn by trial and error how long to leave the pinhole open under different lighting conditions. After you've found the best exposure time for making good pinhole pictures, you can experiment to find the effect of such variables as the pinhole size, number of pinholes, and length of box on the images formed on the film.

PINHOLES THAT AREN'T ROUND • Do you think a pinhole has to be round to make a pinhole image? To find out, make tiny square and triangular pinholes in the centers of several sheets of black paper. If you use these "pinholes" to make pinhole images of the sun, can you still get the sun's image on a second card held below the pinhole? Is the image round? Will these pinholes provide good pinhole images of a light bulb or a candle flame?

A TV STROBOSCOPE • Strobe lights, commonly associated with musical concerts, are often used in science to analyze motion. A *stroboscope*—a rotating slotted disk—mounted in front of a camera with its shutter open can provide a periodic photographic record of a rapidly moving object on film. A flashing strobe light, if sufficiently bright, can serve the same purpose.

A stroboscope can be used to make some moving things appear to stand still. A television screen can be used as a stroboscope; so can a computer screen. Have a friend wave a plastic ruler back and forth in front of a lighted television or computer screen. You'll see that the ruler appears to be "stopped" in several different positions.

You've probably seen the same effect in a movie. Sometimes a wagon wheel in a western appears not to turn as it moves along the road. It may even appear to be turning backward. The wheel will appear to be stationary if the movie camera takes a picture at the same frequency that the wheel is turning. However, the frequencies need not be identical. Suppose, for example, that the wheel has eight identical spokes. If the camera takes a picture every time the wheel makes one-eighth of a rotation, the wheel will also appear stopped because usually we can't tell one spoke from another. So the wheel appears stopped if the camera is taking pictures at the same frequency that the wheel is rotating or if its frequency is eight times, four times, or twice that of the wheel.

What happens if the camera's frequency is less than the wheel's? How do the camera and wheel frequencies compare when the wheel appears to turn slowly backward? Slowly forward? Why does a television or computer screen act like a stroboscope?

A HOMEMADE, HAND-HELD STROBOSCOPE • You can make a stroboscope of your own quite easily. You'll need some cardboard, a spike or a large nail, and a pair of shears. Figure 15 shows you how to use these materials to make the stroboscope. Follow the steps as described below.

Step 1. Cut a circle with a diameter of about 25 cm from a sheet of cardboard.

Step 2. Draw two lines at right angles to each

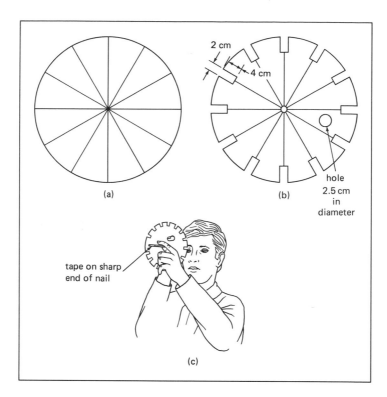

Figure 15. Making a stroboscope.

other. Then divide each quarter circle into 30° intervals. Draw the radii. You have now divided the circle into twelve equal parts as shown in Figure 15a.

Step 3. Cut slots about 2 cm wide and about 4 cm long at the end of each radius, as shown in Figure 15b.

Step 4. Push a spike or a big nail through the center of the disk. **Cover the sharp end with tape.**

Step 5. Cut a hole 2.5 cm in diameter in one of the sections about halfway between the center and the circumference of the disk. See Figure 15b.

Step 6. Hold the strobe firmly by the spike with one hand while you turn it with the index finger of your other hand. Look through the slots.

You can use your stroboscope to determine the rotating frequency of a fan. **Be sure to use a small inexpensive plastic fan that can be safely stopped by hand, or another type of fan that is safely covered with a protective screen.** Before you connect the fan to an electric outlet, put a piece of tape on one blade of the fan. The color of the tape should contrast with the blade so it can be easily identified and singled out from the other blades. Without the tape, if it's a four-bladed fan, you can't tell one blade from another. Now plug in the fan and set it at its slowest speed. Be sure the fan is in bright light because when you turn the strobe in front of your face you'll reduce the intensity of the light reaching your eyes.

Adjust the rate at which you turn the strobe until it appears that you have stopped the fan blade. If you can't turn slowly enough to match the fan's rotation rate, you can cover some of the openings in the disk with tape. (If you do this, be sure the openings that remain are evenly spaced.) Now it's possible to "stop" the fan with a strobe rate that is half the fan's rate of rotation. You may be seeing the blade on every second rotation (or every third or fourth). To find out whether the two rates are exactly matched, double the rate at which you turn the strobe. If the two rates were the same before, you'll now see the blade at *two* stopped positions, one at each half of a turn. Why?

Once you are sure the frequencies of fan and strobe are the same, have someone time how long it takes you to make a certain number of turns with the strobe, say, twenty. Suppose it takes 15 seconds for you to make twenty rotations using a strobe that has twelve evenly spaced viewing slots. You saw 12 × 20 views in 15 seconds. This means the fan must be rotating at a rate of:

$$\frac{12 \times 20 \text{ rotations}}{15 \text{ seconds}} = 16 \text{ rotations/second.}$$

You can use your strobe to look at, "stop," and measure the frequency of other periodic types of motion. For example, you might look at drops of water falling from a faucet, the vibrating clapper on a bell, or a rapidly turning bicycle wheel. What other motions can you stop with your homemade, hand-held stroboscope? What kinds of motion can't you stop with a strobe? You'll find some additional uses for this device in the next chapter.

4
PARTICLES AND WAVES: MODELS OF LIGHT

Scientists enjoy discovering how the world works. If you've enjoyed investigating the properties of light, then you probably will find scientific inquiry interesting and fun. Perhaps, like many scientists, you'll want to go beyond discovering how the world works and try to understand what it is that makes things, and light in particular, behave the way they do.

Attempting to explain what it is about light that makes it reflect and refract as it does requires the development of a theory of light. Scientists agree that a good theory of light, like any good theory, should do two things: It should enable us to explain the properties of light, and it should allow us to predict how light will behave in novel circumstances. Scientific models are not concrete things like model cars. They are creations of the human mind designed to help us better understand some aspect of our world. Nevertheless, real objects are sometimes used to serve as analogies for a model. For example, if we think the behavior of light can be explained by thinking of light as if it consisted of tiny, fast-moving particles, then we could use billiard balls to illustrate how a particle of light might be reflected or refracted. That doesn't mean we believe light is made up of tiny billiard balls. We simply use the billiard balls to create a concrete analogy to show how light particles might bounce or bend when they move from one substance to another.

Common sense tells us that if light is particlelike, the particles are not billiard balls, marbles, or baseballs. Light particles must be much smaller than such objects, and they must travel at very high speeds. In fact, we know that the speed of light in a vacuum is 300,000 kilometers/second (km/s.) If light consists of tiny particles, they are moving so fast that we would never see their paths bend as a result of gravity the way a baseball does after being thrown. In crossing the earth's entire diameter (12,800 km), these speedy light particles would be bent only 9 mm, assuming they accelerate toward earth as other particles do.

A PARTICLE MODEL OF LIGHT • Let's see whether a particle model can explain light. We'll start by investigating reflection.

REFLECTION ○ Tape a sheet of white paper to a smooth tabletop next to a wall as shown in Figure 16. Cover the sheet with a piece of soft-grain carbon paper. Let a steel ball roll down a slightly inclined grooved ruler so it crosses the paper and strikes the wall at an angle and is reflected. The path of the ball rolling over the carbon paper will be recorded on the white sheet. You should be able to see this record by removing the carbon paper.

Repeat the experiment for several different angles. Then measure the ball's angle of incidence and reflection for each case. Are the angles of incidence and reflection nearly the same? Do these particles reflect in the same way that light does? The steel ball represents a particle of light in this analogy. What does the wall represent? How would your experimental results differ if the wall were very rough?

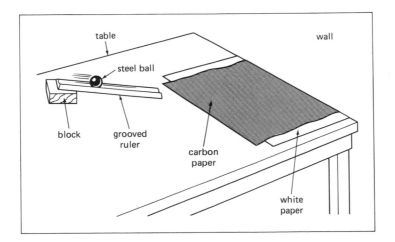

Figure 16. Reflecting particles: an analogy for the particle model of light.

REFRACTION ○ To see whether particles can be made to refract the way light does, you can develop an analogy similar to one that Newton devised about 300 years ago. Place a book on a flat, level table. Find a piece of cardboard a little wider than the book. With a sharp knife, make a slit along one side so that part of the cardboard can be folded as shown in Figure 17. The folded part should be a little wider than the thickness of the book. It will form a ramp from the book to the tabletop.

Tape a sheet of paper to the cardboard that is over the book. Tape another sheet of paper to the table at the base of the ramp. Cover both sheets with carbon paper. In this way the path of a steel ball that rolls down a ruler onto the top of the cardboard-covered book can be recorded. Gravity acting along the ramp provides the force needed to change the path of the ball. It represents the force of attraction between light particles and matter that causes the particle to change its direction of motion. In other words, the particle model suggests that light is bent when it passes from air into water, glass, or any other refracting medium because light particles are attracted to these substances when they are very close to them.

Let a steel ball roll down the grooved ruler as shown in Figure 17. The ball represents a particle of light. It reaches the cardboard ramp, which represents the surface of a medium such as glass or water, at some angle. There it receives a pull from the surface. (In this analogy the pull comes from gravity as the ball rolls down the ramp.) It enters the new medium (the paper on

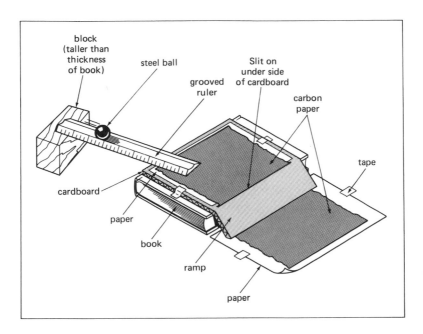

**Figure 17. Refracting particles:
an analogy for the
particle model of light.**

the tabletop in this analogy) at some new angle—the angle of refraction.

Make a few runs at different angles. After each run, remove the carbon paper and carefully identify the path followed by the ball in each medium (upper and lower). You can label the paths with numbers corresponding to the run. When you've completed the experiment, draw the normals. Then measure the angle of incidence (on the upper level) and the angle of refraction (on the lower level) for each run.

Compare the angle of incidence with the angle of refraction for each run. Is the angle of incidence always bigger than the angle of refraction as it was for light? In this analogy the upper level represents air; what might the lower level represent? With care, you can do this experiment quantitatively, but it requires very level surfaces and a constant release height for the ball.

Can you use this same apparatus to show that there is a critical angle for particles passing from the lower level to the upper level? What would the particle model predict about the speed of light in glass or water as compared with the speed of light in air?

PROBLEMS WITH THE PARTICLE MODEL OF LIGHT •

From the analogy you just finished, you can see that a light particle speeds up when its path is bent by the attracting force of the material it is about to enter. This is what makes the angle of refraction less than the angle of incidence according to the particle model. The model leads us to predict that the speed of light will increase when light passes from air to glass or from air to water. Has this prediction ever been tested?

Prior to the nineteenth century, no one had been able to measure the speed of light with accuracy in any medium, not even air. But in 1849, the French physicist Armand Fizeau measured the speed of light in air. In 1853, another Frenchman, Jean Foucault, improved the accuracy of Fizeau's method and succeeded in measuring the speed of light in water as well as in air. He showed that the speed of light actually *decreases* when it passes from air into water. Something is wrong with the model. It predicts the speed of light will increase when light refracts in going from air into water. But experiment shows just the opposite to be true. Now, nature isn't wrong! The theory is wrong!

Because Newton, widely regarded as the greatest genius who ever lived, had been a strong proponent of the particle model, it had been the accepted model among scientists for more than a century. But Foucault's experiment was one of several that led scientists to seriously question the well-established particle model of light during the nineteenth century.

As is common in science, an alternative model soon replaced the particle model of light. The model was not a new one. It had been proposed in the seventeenth century by Christian Huygens, a Dutch scientist who was a contemporary of Newton.

A WAVE MODEL FOR LIGHT • Huygens had suggested that the properties of light could best be explained by a wave model. Before we dismiss Huygens as Newton did, we might examine waves more closely and see whether they can explain the behavior of light.

To begin, let's look at waves moving along a rope or a spring. Have a friend hold one end of a long rope firmly in place (or you can tie the end to a rigid support) while you produce a wave pulse at the other end by moving your hand up and down quickly. The wave, as you can see, will move along the rope. In what direction does the wave travel? How does the direction of motion of the wave compare with the direction that individual parts of the rope move?

We know that light can be reflected. Is a pulse on a rope reflected when it reaches the other, stationary end of the rope? Does the tension in the rope affect the speed at which the wave pulse travels? Can you send horizontal as well as vertical pulses?

Try moving your hand in a circle. Can you send out waves that move in all directions, that is, waves that travel like a corkscrew?

WAVES ON A SLINKY • If possible, obtain a long Slinky. Put the Slinky on a smooth floor and ask a friend to hold one end stationary while you generate pulses at the other end. Does the speed of the pulse depend on the tension in the Slinky? (You can increase the tension by pulling together some of the coils.) If the speed of waves on a stretched Slinky represents a light wave in air, what might the speed of the wave on a less stretched Slinky represent?

Does the speed of the pulse depend on its shape? Does the speed of the pulse change when it is reflected? What can you do to find out?

Have your friend send a pulse at the same time you do so the pulses meet in the middle of the Slinky. Try to make both pulses as similar in size and shape as possible. Do waves pass through each other as beams from different search lights do? What happens to the size of the pulse when two of them collide? Because the pulses move so fast, it's hard to see exactly what happens without using high-speed photography. However, there is a way to determine what happens when the pulses collide.

Have a third person make a rough estimate of how far your pulse moves the Slinky sideways at the midpoint between you and your friend. Have him or her place a few insulated coffee cups upside down on the floor along a line just a bit farther out than the maximum sideways motion of the wave pulse you generate. If you generate a wave, the Slinky should almost, but not quite, touch the cups when the wave passes them. The same should be true of a pulse generated by your friend. Now see what happens when you and your friend generate the same size pulses at the same time on the same side of the Slinky. You'll see the cups at the place where the waves collide fly away when the Slinky hits them. What happens to the size of the pulse at the point where the two pulses overlap?

How should the coffee cups be arranged to find out what happens when pulses of the same size meet if they are on opposite sides of the Slinky? Can you predict what will happen?

Tie a rope or a long, heavy spring to one end of the Slinky. Have your friend hold the far end of the rope or heavy spring while you generate a pulse along the Slinky. Is the pulse transmitted to the rope or heavy spring? Is the speed of the pulse in the heavy spring or rope the same as it is in the Slinky? How is this like the refraction of light? Is all of the pulse transmitted or is some of it reflected? Look at the photograph of light beams passing into a glass block on page 29. Notice that some light is reflected and some is refracted. Does a wave model or a particle model better explain the partial reflection and partial refraction of light passing from one medium to another?

Now have your friend generate a pulse in the heavy spring or rope. What happens when the pulse travels the other way?

WAVES IN TWO DIMENSIONS: A RIPPLE TANK • With a Slinky, you can show that waves reflect (bounce back) and refract (change speed) as does light. However, to see what happens when waves pass from one substance to another at different angles, you will need more than a Slinky.

A ripple tank will allow you to see the motion of waves in two dimensions. You may be able to borrow a ripple tank from your school. If not, you can build one if you have carpentry skills. One simply built tank is shown in Figure 18 together with other materials that can be used with it. The letters used below refer to parts of the tank shown in Figure 18. An old storm window, skylight, or rigid plastic cover A can serve as the transparent bottom for the tank. It can be placed in a wooden frame B (supported by wooden legs) that has been painted with waterproof sealer. The junction of the frame and window should be covered with a sealant such as the kind used around bathtubs (see inset).

Above the center of the tank, build a frame to support a long wooden dowel C, which can be used to support a clear light bulb D and its socket E. Use tape F to fasten the light cord G to the dowel. Near one side of the tank, build a smaller frame to support a smooth, wooden wave generator H. Mount a small battery-powered motor I near the top center of the wave generator. An eccentric on the motor's shaft will cause the generator to vibrate and produce waves. Eyehooks J in the bottom of the frame and the top of the wave generator are used to suspend the wave generator by rubber bands K. Insulated wires L from the motor lead to a low-

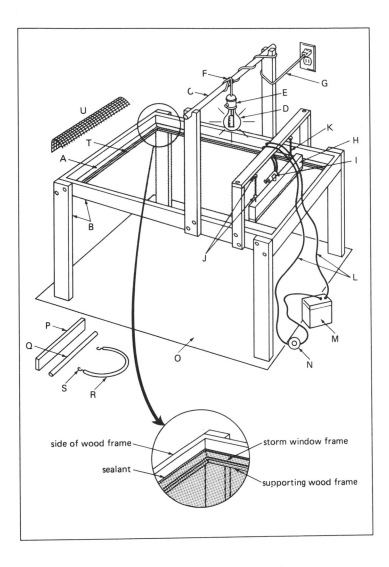

side of wood frame

storm window frame

sealant

supporting wood frame

**Figure 18. A ripple tank
and accessories.
Labels are explained
in the text.**

voltage source of direct current—a dry cell or a power supply M. A rheostat N in the circuit to the battery will allow you to control the motor's speed and thereby the rate at which waves are produced.

A paper screen O beneath the tank will make the wave patterns more visible. A piece of wood P can be used to reflect waves and serve as a "mirror." A dowel Q can be used to produce single wave pulses, and a rubber tube R mounted over a heavy wire S can be used as a curved "mirror."

Once the tank is built, you can add water T and begin looking at wave patterns. To reduce annoying, unwanted reflections from the sides of the tank, you can fold some window screening into V-shaped strips U that fit along the sides of the tank. When covered with cloth gauze, these strips will absorb the waves that strike them.

If you can't borrow a ripple tank, and you don't have the materials or skills to build one, you can use a large, shallow glass baking dish or a rigid plastic sweater box supported by two chairs and still do some of the experiments that follow.

Fill the tank to a depth of about 1 cm with clear water. Measure the depth in various places in the tank to be sure it is level. If it's not level, shim up the low side of the tank. If the tank doesn't have wave absorbers along its sides, you can make some by covering strips of bent wire screening with gauze or thin cloth. Placing these around the edges of the tank will prevent the reflection of unwanted waves.

Be careful not to splash any water on the hot bulb fastened to the supporting dowel above the tank.

Do not attempt to turn the light on or off while your hands are wet. Be sure to wear safety goggles while you work with the ripple tank.

Dip your finger into the water at the center of the tank. You'll see an image of the wave pulse on the screen beneath the tank. The convex-shaped wave crest refracts light and brings it together to produce a bright circular line of light on the screen. Does the wave pulse travel with equal speed in all directions? How do you know?

To make a straight wave, you can use a wooden dowel that is almost as long as the tank is wide. Let the dowel rest on the bottom of the tank. Place the fingers of one hand on top of the dowel and *gently* roll it back toward you a small fraction of a turn. You should see a reasonably straight wave front on the screen. The wave front can be thought of as a large number of rays in a broad bundle moving parallel to each other in the same direction that the wavefront is moving.

REFLECTING WAVES • To find out whether the reflection of water waves is similar to the reflection of light, place a long block of wood on edge near one side of the tank. The block should be big enough that it doesn't float. The surface of the block represents a mirror. With your dowel, send a straight wave pulse perpendicular to the surface of the "mirror" (Figure 19). Is the pulse reflected? Is it reflected straight back the way light would be from a mirror?

Now send some wave pulses into the "mirror" at an angle. How does the angle of reflection compare with the angle of incidence? It's difficult to measure these angles accurately, but you can easily check in other ways to see

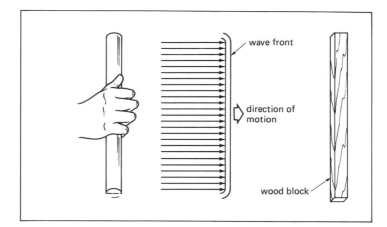

Figure 19. The setup for investigating the reflection of water waves.

whether the waves reflect the way light does. For example, use an eyedropper or your finger to generate a circular pulse in front of the wooden block mirror. This circular pulse could represent one wave pulse coming from a point of light. Watch to see how the wave is reflected. Can you locate the virtual image of the point of light? Is it behind the mirror the way the images were in Chapter 1? What happens to the position of the image if the source of the waves moves farther from the mirror? Closer to the mirror?

On the basis of your observations and experiments do you think a wave model satisfactorily explains reflection?

REFRACTING WAVES • The speed at which water waves travel depends on the depth of the water. In very shallow water they move slowly; in deep water they move faster.

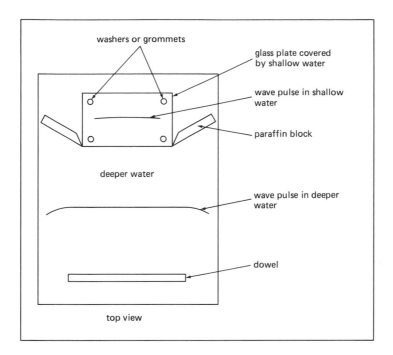

Figure 20. The refraction of a straight wave passing from deep to shallow water.

Thus two depths of water in a ripple tank can represent two substances in which light moves at different speeds—air and glass, for example. Refer to Figure 20 for the following. To see what happens to a wave when it passes from deep to shallow water, place a glass plate in the ripple tank. Put washers or grommets under its corners to support the plate so that the water above the plate is only about 2 mm deep. The water in the rest of the tank should be about 2 cm deep.

Generate a straight-wave pulse and watch what happens when it passes from the deep into the shallow water. Paraffin blocks at the ends of the edge of the glass plate can be used to screen out confusing reflections that may occur at the corners of the plate.

Turn the glass plate so that the wave will enter the shallow water at an angle. Mark the edge of the glass plate (the boundary between deep and shallow water) on the screen below the tank. Draw a line normal to this boundary on the screen. Think of the pulse as a bundle of rays. Do the rays bend toward the normal or away from it when they enter the shallow water? As you can see, this is the way light bends when it passes into a material where its speed is less, for example, from air into glass.

Normally light doesn't come to us in a single one-wave burst. It is reflected continuously to our eyes from the objects we see. Thus, a more realistic model of refraction consists of periodic waves, waves produced one after the other at equal intervals of time.

PERIODIC WAVES • Wave pulses in a ripple tank move too fast for you to measure their speed. However, if you have a series of regularly repeating (periodic) waves, you can measure their wavelengths and frequency. The product of their wavelength and frequency will give you the speed of the waves. Suppose, for example, that the wavelength seen on the screen is 5 cm and the frequency is eight waves per second. Then in one second, eight waves, each 5 cm long, move away from the source. The first wave will be eight wavelengths from the source after one second. Thus it travels 8 × 5 cm or 40 cm in 1 second as seen on the screen. How could you find the actual velocity of the waves in the tank?

To produce periodic waves, place the wave generator in the tank as shown in Figure 21. Use rubber bands to support the wave generator so it can move up and down with each turn of the motor and produce waves at a frequency equal to that at which the motor turns. The eccentric on the motor will make the water move up and down with the wave generator. A rheostat on or connected to the power source will allow you to vary the frequency of the waves. To obtain the best view of refracting waves, operate the motor at the lowest frequency possible. Adjust the wave generator's depth and angle until you have clear, sharp waves.

(If you don't have a wave generator, you can move a ruler up and down in a regular, repeating fashion at one

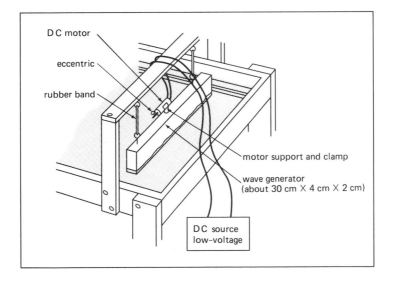

Figure 21. Generating periodic waves.

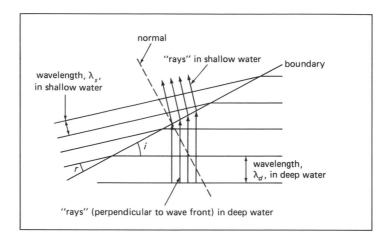

Figure 22. Periodic waves (and rays) approaching and entering shallow water. Can you show that *i* is the angle of incidence and *r* is the angle of refraction?

end of the ripple tank.) Watch what happens when periodic waves, parallel to the boundary, pass from deep to shallow water. Can the frequency of the waves change? Does the wavelength change? Does the speed change? You can see the change in wavelength more clearly if you "stop" the waves with the stroboscope you built in Chapter 3. What is the wavelength of the waves in deep water? In shallow water? Since the frequency is the same in both deep and shallow water, how does the speed of the waves in deep water compare with their speed in shallow water?

If the waves enter the shallow water at an angle, how does the angle of incidence (in deep water) compare with the angle of refraction (in shallow water)?

Remember, you can think of the waves as bundles of rays moving with the wave fronts, as shown in Figure 22. Do these refracting waves behave similarly to the way we'd expect light to behave? As the angle of incidence, i, increases, does the angle of refraction, r, increase too? If you reduce the wavelength, does the degree of refraction change? Is the behavior of light similar to the behavior of waves?

THE REFLECTION OF PERIODIC WAVES ● To see the reflection of these periodic waves, place the wood block you've used as a mirror a few centimeters in front of the wave generator and at an angle to the approaching waves. You have found that for light the angle of incidence is equal to the angle of reflection. Does the angle of reflection of the waves seem to be equal to the angle of incidence?

What do you observe in the region where the incident and reflected waves overlap? This pattern is the result of waves' interacting with one another. It's similar to the way you saw waves add to or cancel one another when you experimented with crossing waves on the Slinky earlier in this chapter. It's an example of what happens when waves from different sources overlap or interfere with each other. It is appropriately called an *interference pattern*. We'll examine interference patterns more closely in Chapter 5.

5
DIFFRACTION AND INTERFERENCE

You know from experience that sound can travel around corners. If a band is marching down Main Street, you can hear it even if you're standing on a side street and can't see the marching musicians. This ability of sound to bend around corners is explained by the *diffraction* of waves—the spreading out of sound waves as they go around corners or through narrow openings. (Unlike the case with light, most eighteenth-century scientists, including Newton, agreed that sound is transmitted in a wave-like fashion. Pulses of high air pressure are established by the vibrating object that makes the sound. These periodic pressure pulses travel through the air to your ear.) Because a gas, such as air, is required to carry sound waves, sound, unlike light, will not travel through a vacuum.

If light is wavelike, we should expect it to diffract too. In this chapter we'll look for diffraction effects with light, but before we start, let's return to the street to consider another observation you can make with sound coming from a marching band. Suppose you're standing on Elm Street, which runs perpendicular to Main, where the band is playing. You'll notice that you can hear the tuba's low-frequency notes, the ones with long wavelengths, quite easily even when the band is far from the intersection of Main and Elm. Except for some reflected waves, you'll hear the high-frequency notes of the flutes and piccolos only when the band is at the intersection. This suggests that the long wavelengths, which come from low-frequency vibrations, diffract more than the short wavelengths which come from high-frequency vibrations.

DIFFRACTION OF WATER WAVES • Place a small piece of paraffin (about a third of a block) or a small wood block in the center of the tank, as shown in Figure 23. Let periodic waves of different wavelengths pass around this small object. Notice how the waves bend (diffract) around the object. Notice that when the wavelength is larger than the object, you wouldn't even know the object was there if you looked at the waves far beyond the object. The waves bend all the way around the object. Could the diffraction of light explain why we

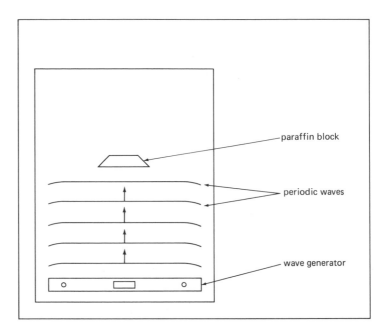

Figure 23. Waves diffracting around an object.

can't see very small things such as tiny particles of dust, soot, and spores that are suspended in air?

If you produce shorter periodic waves, you'll see that the degree of diffraction is reduced. The object begins to cast a "shadow."

Use paraffin blocks to form a narrow opening in the ripple tank, as shown in Figure 24. What happens to a single straight-wave pulse that passes through the opening? The photographs on page 84 show you what to expect when periodic waves pass through a narrow opening.

Now let periodic waves pass through the opening. What happens to the amount of diffraction as the open-

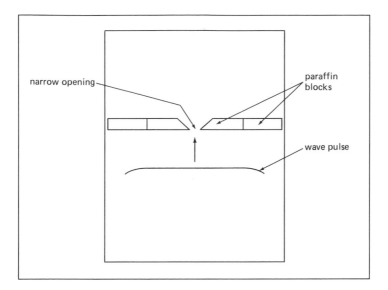

**Figure 24. Waves passing through
a narrow opening.**

ing is made smaller? Larger? What happens if you
change the frequency and thereby the wavelength of the
waves? How is diffraction related to the ratio λ/W? (The
Greek letter λ, lambda, is used to represent the wavelength, and W the width of the slit.)

From this experiment, we see that if light is wavelike, we should expect light to diffract. But for diffraction to occur, how would the size of the slits and objects
have to compare with the wavelength of light?

Use the paraffin blocks to make two narrow slits for
the waves to pass through, as shown in Figure 25.
Notice that the diffraction creates the equivalent of two
point sources of waves beyond the openings. If your

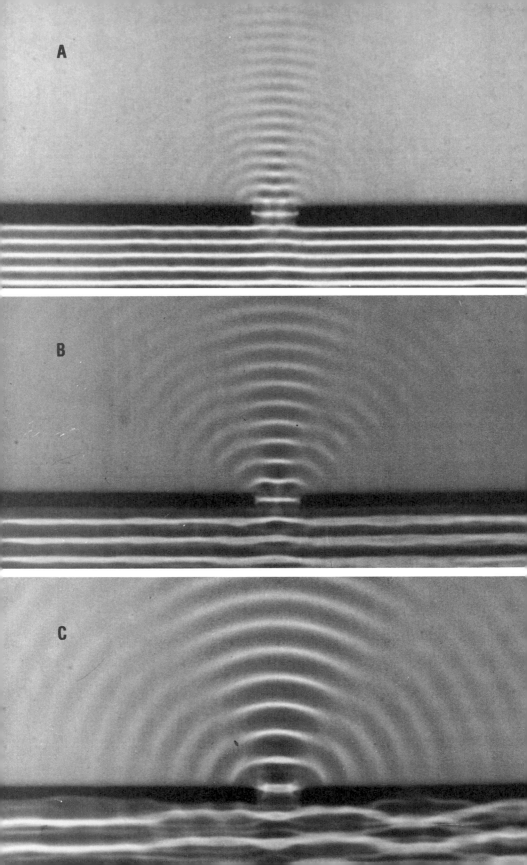

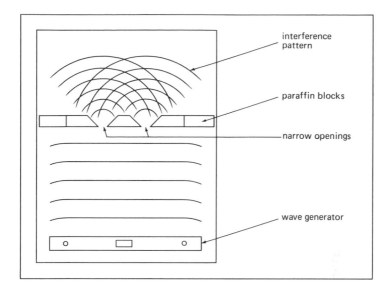

interference
pattern

paraffin blocks

narrow openings

wave generator

**Figure 25. Waves diffracting through two
narrow, closely spaced slits.**

waves are sharp and clear, you should be able to see an
interference pattern in the overlapping diffracted waves.
The regions where the waves cancel are called *nodal
lines*.

Before we go on to look at interference patterns
more closely, let's find out whether we can find any
evidence that light diffracts.

DIFFRACTION OF LIGHT • You've seen waves spread out
in a ripple tank when they pass through a narrow open-

**Water waves diffracting in a ripple tank. As the
wavelength increases from A to B to C, what
happens to the amount of diffraction?**

ing. Let's see whether we can find a similar effect with light by making it pass through a narrow opening. Hold your index and second fingers close together as you look at the vertical line filament of a clear (unfrosted) showcase bulb 1 m away. When the space between your fingers is very narrow, you'll see the light spread out into a series of bright and dark bands like those in the photograph on page 87. Even if you view an ordinary light bulb in this way, you'll be able to see a series of dark lines that run parallel to the narrow opening. If you bring the edges of two mirrors close together, you may be able to make a narrower and better-defined opening. Can you see the bright and dark bands that form as the light spreads out?

Light, like waves in a ripple tank, spreads out when it passes through very narrow openings. With light, the opening has to be very small for us to see the diffraction effect. What does this tell us about the wavelength of light?

INTERFERENCE OF WATER WAVES • Now that we've seen evidence that light does indeed diffract when it passes through very small openings, let's look at interference patterns in the ripple tank. Then we can go on to look for a similar pattern with light.

To see more clearly the pattern that forms when two point sources of waves overlap, you can use two point sources of waves attached to the ripple bar in place of the two slits you used earlier to make an interference pattern in the ripple tank. Figure 26 shows such an arrangement. (If you don't have small plastic spheres and connecting right-angle rods that fit into holes in the wave generator

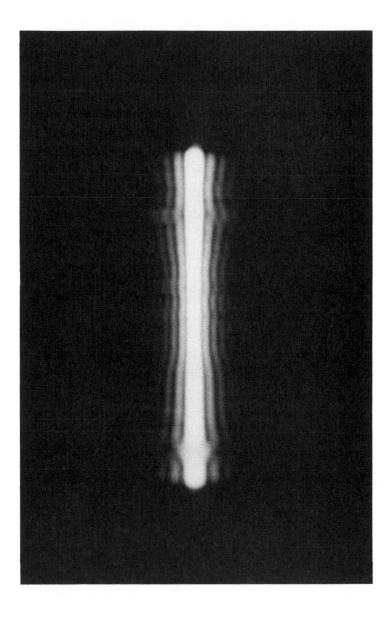

The interference pattern seen here was made by light passing through a single narrow slit.

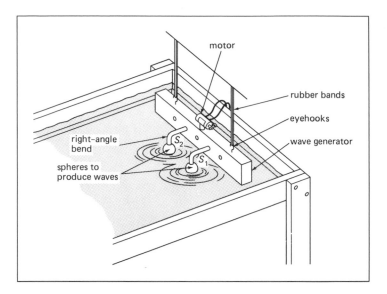

Figure 26. Two point sources of waves, S_1 and S_2, produce interference patterns when they generate waves together.

as shown, you can make a pair. Use epoxy glue to attach two marbles to a pair of bent nails or design your own point sources for making waves.

Produce an interference pattern in your tank like the one shown in the photograph on page 89. Notice the waves extending outward from between the two sources of waves, S_1 and S_2. The bright, nearly parallel lines are the maxima where crests from S_1 meet crests from S_2. Troughs from the same two sources also meet along these same lines. Between the bright lines we see nodal lines where the waves from the two sources cancel, that is, where the crests from one source are always paired

Water waves from two point sources create an interference pattern in a ripple tank.

with troughs from the other source. These nodal lines can be seen to extend outward from their origin between S_1 and S_2. Figure 27 shows you how the two wave sources produce nodes and maxima in the region between the two wave sources:

1. S_1 and S_2, which are exactly two wavelengths apart, are producing waves in a ripple tank. S_1 has just finished producing a wave crest. Waves from S_1 are indicated by dashes $-----$. (See Figure 27a.)
2. At the same time, S_2 has also just finished producing a wave crest. Waves from S_2 are shown by dots . . . . We will see what happens as the waves move through each other in the region between the two sources. (See Figure 27b.)
3. At this point, where both have just finished producing wave crests, the waves cancel each other. The water surface is flat as shown by the solid line _____, which is the sum of the two waves. This is because the crests from S_1 lie on the troughs from S_2 and vice versa. (See Figure 27c.)

Figure 27. How waves from two sources interfere with each other.

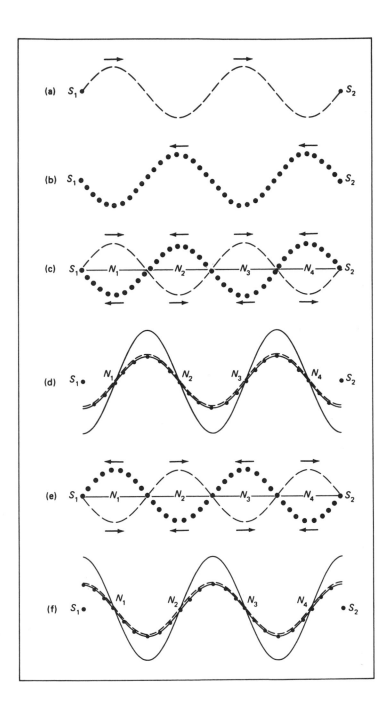

4. Now look at the waves when all the waves have moved one-quarter wavelength. Both sources are midway through producing a trough. Notice how large the water waves are where the crests from the two sources and the troughs from the two sources overlap. (See Figure 27d.)
5. After another quarter-wavelength, both sources have completed producing troughs and the water is again flat between the sources. (See Figure 27e.)
6. After another quarter-wavelength, the wave pattern is similar to one we've seen before except that the large crests and troughs have switched positions. (See Figure 27f.)

Throughout the movement of waves between the two sources, you can see that there has been no motion of the water at points N_1, N_2, N_3, and N_4. These points where the water is always calm are called *nodal points*. Notice that they are half a wavelength apart. At nodal points, the sum of the waves from the two sources is always zero. In a ripple tank these nodal points extend out into the tank as nodal lines. (See Figure 28 and the photograph on page 89.)

If you follow the maxima produced between the two sources outward into the tank, you'll see that each flickering bright line becomes a broad band of waves. Each band is a single maximum. The one that is perpendicular to the line between the sources S_1 and S_2 is called the *central maximum*, or simply the "central max."

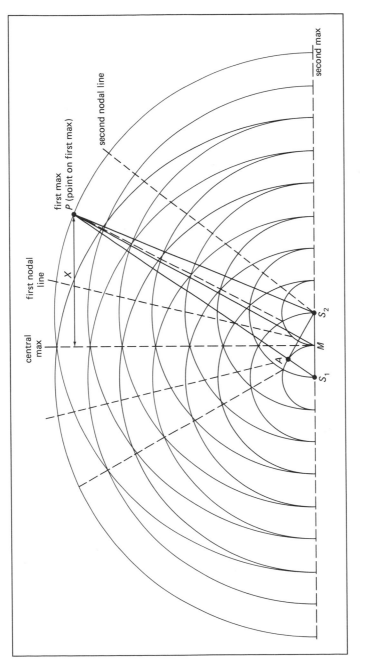

Figure 28. An interference pattern produced by two point sources S_1 and S_2.

The quiet, waveless bands between the maxima are the nodal lines, which can be traced back to the nodes between the sources. Notice that both the nodal lines and the maxima become straight at large distances from the wave sources.

Try changing the pattern. Is it affected by the frequency or wavelength? If so, how is it affected? Is it affected by the distance between the two sources of waves? If so, how? Can you compensate for changes in the frequency by changing the separation of the sources?

If you're familiar with geometry, you can analyze the interference pattern created by two sources of waves and find a way to measure the wavelength of the waves without actually having to see the waves. Since we can't see waves of light, knowing how to measure the wavelength without actually seeing the waves might be helpful if we can find an interference pattern using light.

Establish an interference pattern with three to five nodal lines on each side of the central max. Look at the pattern on the screen below the ripple tank. Pick a point on the center of a maximum that is as far as possible from the sources but still clearly visible. In Figure 28, P is far from the sources. The reason for the large distance is to make the lines PS_1 and PS_2 as close to parallel as possible. The difference in length, $PS_1 - PS_2$ must be one wavelength ($1\,\lambda$) since crests from S_1 and S_2 meet at P. You can check this by counting the number of wavelengths between P and each source S_1 and S_2.

You can use Figure 29 to derive a formula to calculate the wavelength without having to see the waves. In Figure 29 the triangles from Figure 28 have been extracted from the wave patterns to make them more visible. PS_1 and PS_2 are very nearly parallel, and $PA = PS_2$ because AS_1 is the path difference $PS_1 - PS_2$, which is $n\lambda$, where λ is the wavelength.

Triangles $AS_1 S_2$ and CPM are similar because both are right triangles and angle $a = a'$. Since $AS_1 = n\lambda$ (in Figure 28, $n = 1$),

$$\frac{n\lambda}{d} = \frac{X}{L}, \text{ so } \lambda = \frac{dX}{nL}.$$

Measure the distance from the point you picked on a maximum to the center of the line $(S_1 S_2)$ that connects the two sources. (For ease and consistency, measure all distances on the screen.) This distance is L in Figure 29. Also measure the perpendicular distance from the point you picked on the center of the nth max to the center of the central max. This is the distance X in Figure 29. Finally, measure the distance d between the centers of the two sources, which show up as bright spots on the screen. With these three measurements and the information in Figure 29, you should be able to calculate the wavelength of the waves that produced the interference pattern. What do you calculate the wavelength to be?

You can check your calculation by measuring the wavelength on the screen directly. First, be sure the pattern has not changed. If it has, you can use your marks to reestablish the same pattern. Use a paraffin block to reflect the waves at the side of one of the wave sources. The block reflects the waves and acts like another wave source. The incoming and reflected waves will interfere and create nodes and maxima. This pattern

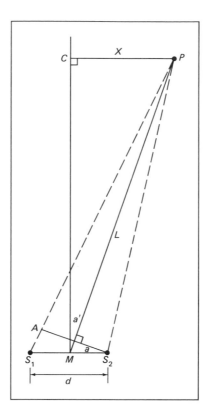

Figure 29. An analysis of an interference pattern.

will allow you to measure the wavelength easily. (Remember, the nodes are half a wavelength apart.) Do the calculated and measured values of the wavelength agree reasonably well?

Repeat the experiment using a different wavelength to create a different interference pattern. What do you find this time?

Now if we can find a way to make a visible interference pattern using light, perhaps we can use the same formula we used here to measure the wavelength of light.

INTERFERENCE OF LIGHT • You've seen that a very narrow opening is required to make light diffract. To establish an interference pattern like the one shown in Figure 28 and in the photograph on page 99 will require two very narrow openings that are close together.

In an experiment performed early in the nineteenth century, Thomas Young placed a fine hair across a pinhole. Each side of the pinhole served as a narrow opening to diffract sunlight coming through a hole in a window shutter into an otherwise darkened room. You'll find it easier to use two narrow slits, as Young did in a later experiment, and an unfrosted (clear) showcase bulb.

To prepare the slits, first use a small artist's brush to coat a microscope slide with a suspension of graphite in alcohol. To make the suspension, stir powdered graphite into alcohol. You can also use a glass photographic plate or the back of a small pocket mirror instead of the coated slide. After the suspension has dried, **ask an adult to prepare the slits.** He or she should take a pair of double-edge razor blades and hold them together side by side. **As a safety precaution, cover the upper set of edges with tape.** Using a ruler as a guide, draw the blades, tipped at a small angle, across the slide as shown in Figure 30. The slits should be one razor blade thickness apart. To find out whether the slits have been made correctly, look at a straight, bright filament in a clear bulb. You should see the light spread out into a series of

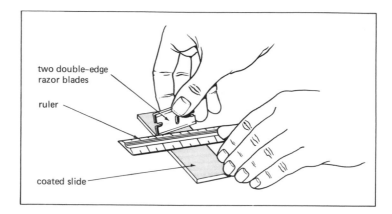

two double-edge
razor blades

ruler

coated slide

Figure 30. Preparing slits to produce an interference pattern.

evenly spaced bright and dark bands. If you see un-evenly spaced bands with a bright, wide band at the center, you have made a single slit. Ask your adult helper to repeat the process, several times if necessary, until you have two slits that produce a clear pattern like the one described above or the one you can see (as a black-and-white pattern) in the photograph on page 99.

The pattern you see through the two slits has a series of bright bands separated by dark lines. Because different colors diffract differently, the colors are spread into a spectrum in each band. To see the pattern more clearly, hold a transparent piece of red, green, or blue plastic or cellophane in front of the slits. Notice the similarity of this pattern to the interference pattern you saw in the ripple tank. The pattern you're seeing is a

Light passing through two narrow and closely spaced parallel slits produces an interference pattern. Note that the maxima (bright bands) and nodal lines (dark lines) are equally spaced as are the ones seen in the previous photograph.

smaller version of what you'd see if you looked horizontally across the surface of an interference pattern in a ripple tank. The dark lines are the nodal lines. The bright bands are the maxima. Our ability to create such a pattern by diffracting light shows that real phenomena can be predicted from the wave model of light.

Now, if you were able to calculate the wavelength of the water waves in the ripple tank, you can make a similar calculation here and find the wavelength of light.

To make this measurement, support a horizontal ruler over the showcase bulb, as shown in Figure 31. Stand about 2 m in front of the bulb and look at the light through the two slits that were made in the slide. The slits and the bulb filament should be parallel. Your eye will automatically place the pattern on the ruler when you focus on it. Have a partner move two white paper markers along the ruler until they are separated by a number of bright bands (maxima) or dark bands (nodal lines) that you can easily count. You'll be able to see both the pattern and the markers if you look partly through and partly over the slits. The distance between the markers corresponds to the X in Figures 28 and 29. The distance between your eye and the ruler is very close to being the L in the same figure, and the distance between the slits is d, the thickness of one razor blade.

You can measure d by using a micrometer to find the thickness of a razor blade. Or you can place the slits in a slide projector and magnify them on a screen. Measure the distance between the slits on the screen. Then replace them with a segment of a clear plastic ruler. By projecting the lines of the ruler on the screen, you will know the magnification factor of the slide projector.

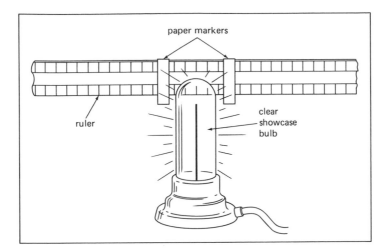

Figure 31. Viewing an interference pattern made when light passes through two narrow, closely spaced slits.

By measuring d, X, and L and counting the number of maxima or nodal lines between the markers to find n, you will be able to calculate the average wavelength of light as Young did. As you can see from the drawings in Figures 28 and 29, if L is large, it changes little from one maximum in the pattern to another. When we go from one maximum to the next, the change in n is simply 1, and so the distance between neighboring maxima or nodes ΔX will be given by

$$\Delta X = \lambda \frac{L}{d}$$

You can use the average value of ΔX to find the wavelength because

$$\lambda = \frac{d \, \Delta X}{L}$$

What do you find the average wavelength of light to be? Young found it was about 0.0005 mm.

If you cover the showcase bulb or the slits with a red, blue, or green filter, what do you find for the wavelength of these different-colored lights?

Which color has the longest wavelength? Which color has the shortest wavelength?

INTERFERENCE PATTERNS USING A DIFFRACTION GRATING • You can buy a plastic diffraction grating in a hobby store or from a science supply company (see appendix) for very little money. You might also be able to borrow one from your school. The slits in a diffraction grating are much closer together than they were on the slide you made. In fact, most of the inexpensive gratings sold by science supply companies have 528 slits per millimeter. This means that d, the distance between the slits, is only 0.0019 mm. By making d so small, we can expect the values of X to be reasonably large. If you look at the showcase bulb filament through such a grating, you will see that the maxima are indeed far apart. With such large values of X, the wavelength can be determined more accurately. What do you find the wavelength of various colors of light to be using a diffraction grating?

A more direct way to measure the wavelength of light with a diffraction grating is to use a slide projector. Remove the film from an old slide you plan to discard, or make a new slide from some thin cardboard. Use black tape to cover most of the opening in the slide, but leave a narrow vertical opening in the middle so that a slit of light coming through the projector lens can be focused on a screen about 1 m away.

Tape a diffraction grating over the lens housing from which the light emerges. Be sure the grating is oriented in such a way that it spreads the light horizontally. You can see maxima on either side of the central max where you have focused the light. It's easy to measure X from the central max on the screen to either of the first maxima on either side. The distance from the grating to the maximum of your choice is L, and you already know d. Choose any color you want and measure its wavelength.

By measuring the X and L values at each end of one spectrum in a maximum, you can determine the range of the wavelengths of visible light that you can see. What's the shortest wavelength you can see? What's the longest wavelength you can see?

If either you or someone you know is color-blind, use this experiment to find the range of wavelengths that a color-blind person can see. Are certain regions of the spectrum invisible to a color-blind person, or are they seen differently than they are by most people?

POISSON'S SPOT • Although Thomas Young used a wave model to explain the interference pattern he made using two narrow slits, his explanation was not taken seriously by his contemporaries. Despite the fact that most scientists disregarded Young's attempt to revive Huygens' wave model of light, a few listened. In 1818, Augustin Fresnel developed a mathematical basis for

Young's wave theory, but Fresnel too encountered overwhelming opposition when he submitted his work for review.

Simon Poisson showed that one consequence of Fresnel's theory was that the diffraction of light around a small disk or sphere should produce a bright spot at the center of the circular shadow cast by such an object. Such a spot had never been observed, and so Poisson thought he had refuted Fresnel's theory. Fresnel, however, tested Poisson's prediction and found that indeed there was a bright spot in the center of the shadow cast by a small disk. You can see Poisson's spot in the photograph on page 105.

To produce Poisson's spot, place a small sphere in the beam from a low-power helium-neon laser. (**Don't look into the laser!**) A small sphere about 2 to 4 mm in diameter when placed at a point in the diverging beam where the beam is wider than the sphere will cast a sharp shadow on a screen.

For a sphere you can use the head of a hat pin or something comparable. Stick the pin into a wooden block and slide it into the laser beam. As an alternative, you can tape a needle to the end of a strong bar magnet and adjust the extension of the needle from the magnet so it will support a small ball bearing hung from it as shown in Figure 32. Place the pinhead or suspended bearing in the beam about 30 cm beyond the lens. You should be able to see the entire circular shadow of the sphere on a white screen or wall a meter or so away. Look carefully at the shadow. Can you find interference fringes around the shadow? Can you find a bright spot of light at the center of the shadow?

The diffraction of light around a small disk produces Poisson's spot, the bright point at the center of the circular shadow cast by the disk.

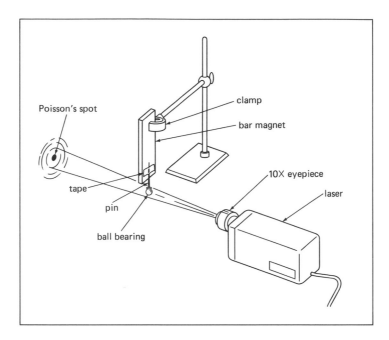

Figure 32. Finding Poisson's spot.

You may see Poisson's spot more clearly if a diverging (concave) lens is placed in front of the laser. Try placing a 10× eyepiece from a microscope in the path of a beam from the laser. The lens will converge the light to a point, after which it will form a diverging beam. Put the sphere into the beam at a point where the beam is wider than the sphere. Does this improve the visibility of the interference pattern and Poisson's spot? Does the pattern improve if a pinhole is placed at a point where the lens converges the laser beam?

6
POLARIZATION

Some waves, such as sound waves, are carried by the back-and-forth movement of the matter through which the sound travels. When you pluck a guitar string, the string vibrates. Its movement pushes on the air around it. Each time it moves to the right, it pushes some air to the right and creates a pulse of high air pressure that moves outward from the string through the air. When it moves to the left, it creates a pressure pulse in the other direction and a low-pressure region on the right. These alternating regions of high and low pressure constitute the sound waves that travel through air.

When they reach your eardrum, they push it in and out, and the change in pressure causes you to hear the sound. Waves, such as sound waves, that move back and forth along the same axis as the matter that carries the waves are called *longitudinal waves*.

Other waves do not move along the same axis as the matter that carries them. A water wave, for example, may move from one end of a swimming pool to the other. But if you're floating in the pool, you simply move up and down like a cork when the wave passes. The water, and anything floating on it, moves up and down while the wave moves horizontally. Waves that move this way are said to be *transverse waves*.

MAKING POLARIZED WAVES • Attach one end of a length of rope to an eyehook fastened to a wall or post. Then, with a quick up-down motion of your hand, shake a pulse along the rope as shown in Figure 33a. This is an example of a *polarized* transverse wave. In such a wave, the transverse motion of the wave is in a single plane. If you shake a pulse into the rope by moving your hand quickly to the side and back, rather than up and down, you'll have a polarized wave at right angles to the first one. Try it! In fact, you can shake the pulse into the rope at any angle between vertical and horizontal. If you move your hand in a small circle, you can make waves that have all the possible axes of transverse motion (Figure 33b).

To polarize a transverse wave moving along all possible axes, such as a turning jump rope, make a slot in a board as shown in Figure 33c. If the slot is oriented vertically, only the vertical part of the rope's wave motion

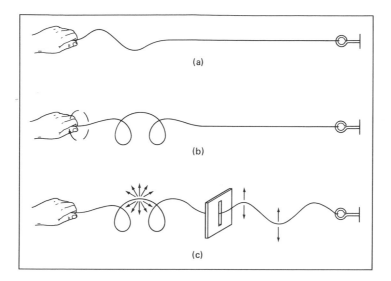

Figure 33. Transverse waves can be generated along any axis perpendicular to the wave's direction of motion.

is transmitted. If the slot is horizontal, only horizontal waves will be transmitted. Waves vibrating in all other directions will be filtered out.

POLARIZED LIGHT • Because light can be polarized, scientists believe light waves are transverse. Although light can be polarized, no material medium such as a rope, water, or air is needed to transmit light. It can even travel through the vacuum of space. A material known by the trade name Polaroid is widely used to polarize light. Polaroid allows light waves to be transmitted primarily along only one axis of the transverse waves.

The Polaroid absorbs most of the energy in the waves oriented in other directions. To see this effect, place one piece of Polaroid on another and look through them toward an open window. If you don't have Polaroid sheets, you can use the lenses from a pair of sunglasses that have Polaroid filters. What happens to the intensity of the light as you rotate one of the two Polaroid filters (polarizers)?

If the axes of the two filters are parallel, both will transmit light. But when the axes of the two Polaroid are at right angles to each other, ideally no light can pass. It would be like having a rope with two slotted boards. If the slots are parallel, waves oriented along the direction of the slots will be transmitted (Figure 34a). If the slots are perpendicular to each other, waves can't pass (Figure 34b). If the axes of two polarizers are at an angle other than 90°, some light will be transmitted.

POLARIZED SKY • Is reflected light polarized? To find out, let light from a window or a light bulb reflect from various surfaces—wood (a wooden desk top is good), glass, metal, paper, water, and other smooth surfaces. Look at the reflected light through a polarizer. Which materials partially polarize the reflected light? Which seem to have little or no effect? If possible, take your polarizer outside and look at sunlight reflected from various surfaces. **Be sure not to look at the sun or its reflected image.** Does the angle at which the light is reflected to your eye have any effect on the amount of light that is polarized? Do you see why it's advisable for automobile drivers to wear polarized sunglasses on sunny days?

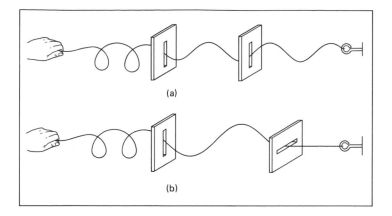

Figure 34. Making polarized waves on a rope.

Look at a patch of blue sky about 90° from the sun through a Polaroid sheet or a lens from Polaroid sunglasses. The effect is best seen when the sun is low in the sky, the air is dry, and little dust or pollution is in the air. Turn the Polaroid. You'll see a distinct change in the intensity of the light. What does this tell you about light from the sky? What do you observe when you repeat the experiment while looking at light at different angles from the sun? **Don't look at the sun or the sky near the sun. Such intense light can seriously damage your eyes.**

Try the experiment with colored filters in front of the Polaroid. Does the light's color affect the amount of light removed by the polarizer?

Is the light reflected from clouds polarized? Is light from the moon polarized? Design an experiment to find out.

For black-and-white photographs, photographers often use a filter to obtain good contrast between white clouds and blue sky. Take some of your own black-and-white photographs of the sky. What color filter provides the best contrast? Can you explain why?

Take some *color* photographs of the sky. Do you get better photographs with a Polaroid filter?

The polarization of sky light is the result of scattering by tiny particles in the atmosphere. The sunlight absorbed by these particles is reradiated in all directions. From earlier experiments, you may know that the wavelength of blue light is shorter than the wavelength of other visible colors. Since shorter wavelengths are scattered significantly more than longer wavelengths, the color of the scattered light is predominantly blue. This scattered light is reflected, absorbed, and reradiated by other particles in the air, giving us a background of blue. Consequently, the light coming from the sky appears to be blue. The sun appears yellow rather than white because the atmosphere scatters much of the blue light before it reaches the ground.

A VIEW OF SCATTERED AND UNSCATTERED LIGHT ● To see scattered light, place a glass of water near a light bulb and look at the light going through the water from the side. You'll see very little reflected light, but if you look at the bulb through the water, you'll see it quite clearly because most of the light is transmitted by the water. Now add a small amount of powdered nondairy creamer or a few drops of milk to the water and stir. What happens when you view the light from the side of the glass now? What color is the reflected light? Look directly at the bulb through the water again. Is the color of the transmitted light different than it was before? What happens to the quantity and color of the light scattered to the side as more milk or powder is added? What happens to the apparent color of the bulb when viewed directly through the water?

Would you expect the transmitted light to be polarized? How about the reflected light? What do you find when you test with a polarizer?

You can do this same experiment on a grander scale by shining the light from a slide projector through an aquarium filled with water. Adding small increments of powdered nondairy creamer to the water will simulate the color changes seen at sunset. From the side, you can see the light scattered by the tiny particles in the water. A polarizer will reveal that the scattered light is polarized.

HAIDINGER'S BRUSH • You can detect polarized light with your eyes if you look carefully. Place a piece of white paper in bright, natural light—a kitchen counter illuminated by a nearby window is good. Look at the center of the paper through a polarizer held close to one eye for a few seconds. Then rotate the Polaroid 90° and look closely. You will see a faint yellow hourglass figure with a bluish tint on either side of the yellow. This is Haidinger's brush, named after the Austrian mineralogist who discovered the phenomenon in 1844. Notice how the figure turns with the rotation of the Polaroid. The effect is believed to be due to chemicals in the center of the retina (the fovea) that absorb polarized blue light. If the light is polarized horizontally, the light is absorbed vertically, giving a vertical, yellow hourglass because the complementary color of blue is yellow.

Go outside and look at a patch of blue sky about 90° from the sun. Try it first without a Polaroid filter. **Don't look at the sun or the sky near the sun.** You may be able to see Haidinger's brush. Some people can see it quite clearly. Others can't see it at all. Now try it using the polarizer as you did when you looked at the figure on white paper. Does this help?

ROTATING THE PLANE OF POLARIZATION • Some materials rotate the plane of polarized light. These materials include cellophane wrappers, cellophane tape (the kind that looks yellow and is generally the least expensive), mylar, solid plastics, and glass under stress. You can test a variety of materials for this characteristic property quite easily. Hold the material between two polarizers and observe the transmitted light as you rotate one of the polarizers. Look for changes in the color of the transmitted light. The photograph on page 115 shows a transparent object under stress and viewed through Polaroids. The dark areas are relatively unstressed. The greatest stress occurs where the pattern changes from light to dark.

The amount the polarized light is rotated depends on the thickness of the material and the wavelength of the light. Certain thicknesses will rotate a particular wavelength just enough so that it can pass through the second filter. Other wavelengths will be partially or totally absorbed. As a result, the colors that you see change as the polarizer is turned.

You can make an interesting and beautiful display

Viewed through Polaroids, the stress patterns in a piece of transparent material squeezed in a vise are apparent. The relatively unstressed areas are dark. The greatest stress occurs where the pattern changes from light to dark.

using this property characteristic of some materials. To a large glass plate, tape a variety of materials that rotate polarized light such as pieces of sandwich bags and a variety of pieces of broken, transparent plastic. Be sure the tape you use rotates polarized light. Place the glass plate near a bright window between two polarizers. Rotate one of the polarizers and watch the colorful and changing patterns. Alternatively, you can make a polarizing kaleidoscope. Pile a bunch of these pieces of material on a clear sheet of glass or plastic and support the sheet safely above a light source. Then place a Polaroid sheet below the display and another above it. By rotating the upper piece of Polaroid, you can view the colors of the transmitted light.

ROTATING POLARIZED LIGHT WITH KARO SYRUP • To see the effect of wavelength on the rotation of polarized light by a thick solution of sugar, let light from a nearby bulb shine through a bottle of clear Karo syrup. Place a polarizer on each side of the syrup. You can use a clothespin to hold the polarizer closer to the bulb while you rotate the other one in front of your eye. See how the colors change as you rotate the polarizer. What colors do you see?

Hold a mirror between your eye and the polarizer you are rotating. By carefully adjusting the mirror, you should be able to split the light beam that comes through the second polarizer. In this way you'll be able to see reflected light as well as light that comes directly from the polarizer to your eye. Rotate the polarizer and compare the colors of the reflected and unreflected light.

What do you find? Are the two colors always the same? Are they ever the same?

If you have a small, clear plastic box and a prism, place the prism on the bottom of the box and fill the box with Karo syrup. Support the box above a light source. Then place a piece of Polaroid below the box and rotate a second polarizer above the box. What type of color patterns do you see as you rotate the polarizer?

7
PHOTOELECTRICITY

Experiments involving the interference of light early in the nineteenth century eventually led scientists to replace the particle model of light with the wave model. At the end of the same century, experiments with photoelectricity led scientists to question the wave model of light and to develop a new, modified particle model.

In 1888, the German physicist Heinrich Hertz and others found that if plates of zinc, copper, and silver were charged negatively, they would readily discharge when exposed to the short wavelengths of ultraviolet light—the invisible light that tans your skin. However, the longer wavelengths of visible light would not discharge such metals. Later they found that chemically active metals such as sodium, potassium, and cesium could be discharged by visible light as well as ultraviolet light.

This ability of light to transfer its energy to charged particles was called the photoelectric effect. You can examine this effect experimentally.

THE PHOTOELECTRIC EFFECT ● To investigate the photoelectric effect as Hertz did, you will need an *electroscope,* a device that can detect and measure electric charge. If you don't have access to an electroscope, you can make one similar to the one in Figure 35. A thin sheet of zinc about 8 cm square can be used as a plate for the electroscope. Be sure to clean the zinc surface with steel wool or emery paper. **Ask an adult to help you drill a hole** in the center of the zinc plate. For the experiment to work, the air must be dry. The experiment cannot be done on a hot and humid day.

To charge the electroscope, rub a comb, a test tube, or a plastic ruler with a paper towel or a wool cloth. Then touch the zinc plate with the charged object. You may hear a spark jump when charge is transferred from the charged object to the electroscope. Once the electroscope is charged, the aluminum foil strips will repel each other and spread apart, as shown in the photograph on page 121. Why?

To see what happens when charge is removed from the electroscope, simply light a match and hold it near the zinc plate. The flame will produce ions (charged atoms) in the air around the plate. Ions that carry a charge opposite in sign to the excess charge on the

119

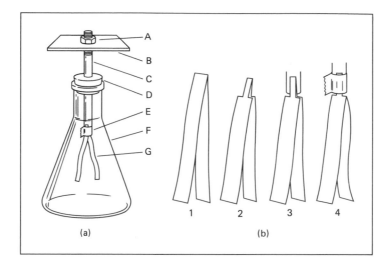

Figure 35. An electroscope. (a) Parts of the electroscope: A—Nut to fasten zinc plate to rod. B—Zinc plate (both sides cleaned with cleansing pad). C—Metal rod with threaded end. (Clean both ends with scouring pad.) D—Rubber stopper with single hole. E—Tape to fasten aluminum leaves to rod. F—glass flask. G—Electroscope leaves—strips of aluminum foil. (b) To make the leaves: 1. Fold strip of aluminum foil. 2. Cut narrow strip at top. 3. Place narrow strip on bottom of metal rod. 4. Tape aluminum to metal rod. Be sure leaves and rod make good contact.

**Why are the leaves of this
electroscope spread apart?**

electroscope will be attracted to the zinc and neutralize it.

Recharge the electroscope and shine an ultraviolet light on the zinc plate. A low-intensity "black light" or a small ozone or mercury lamp is safe as long as you don't look directly at the light. **If you use other sources of ultraviolet light, wear protective glasses to filter out ultraviolet light.** If the electroscope discharges quickly, what was the sign of the charge on the zinc plate? If it doesn't discharge quickly, you must have put an excess of positive charge on the electroscope. In either case, you can give the electroscope a charge opposite in sign to the one it had if you charge it by induction.

Charging by induction means that you should *induce* charge to move onto the electroscope. You can use the charged object you used before (comb, ruler, or test tube) to do this. The charged body will attract charges *opposite* in sign to its own charge. In this way you will give the electroscope a charge opposite in sign to the charge it had before. To induce charge on the electroscope, place a finger on the zinc plate. Then use your other hand to bring the charged body *near* (**don't touch**) the zinc plate. Charge from the earth can move through your body and finger to the zinc plate. If the charge that is doing the attracting is negative in sign, then positive charge will collect on the zinc plate and spread over the entire electroscope. If the attracting charge is positive, then the electroscope will acquire a negative charge. Now remove your finger from the zinc plate. *After* you remove your finger, move the charged body away from the electroscope.

Why should you remove your finger *before* you

move the charged object? Why did the aluminum leaves repel only *after* you had removed *both* your finger and the charged object?

The electroscope now carries a charge opposite in sign to the charge it carried before. What do you think will happen when you shine ultraviolet light on the zinc plate now? Now that you know how to charge an electroscope, design an experiment to find out whether an ordinary incandescent bulb will discharge a negatively charged electroscope. What do you conclude? Do you think infrared light will discharge the electroscope? How can you find out?

Suppose you cover an ultraviolet light source with a glass plate before you hold it near the negatively charged zinc plate. What happens this time? What does this tell you about the glass? Could you get a suntan inside a greenhouse?

PHOTOELECTRIC CELLS IN YOUR HOME • There are probably photoelectric cells, often called electric eyes, in your home and in the stores where you shop. When you walk into a supermarket, the door springs open as if by magic. As dusk falls, you may notice the lights go on in a neighbor's house even though you know the family is not at home. The night light in your own hallway or room may go on at night even though you have not touched it. All of these mechanisms work because light can transfer its energy to electric charge. The energy provided by the light makes the charge move and gives rise to an electric current, which can be amplified and used to control switches. Photoelectric devices used to consist of metallic surfaces mounted in a vacuum tube.

Today, solid-state photocells have replaced vacuum tubes, but the principle is still the same—light energy is transferred to electric charges.

A light source shines on a photocell, producing a current. The current is amplified and sent through a relay. As long as light shines on the photocell, a current flows through an electromagnet in the relay that attracts a switch keeping another circuit open. If the light beam is interrupted by someone's crossing the beam, or by darkness, the photoelectric current is shut off. The current through the electromagnet drops to zero, and the switch it controls closes, creating a current in another circuit that controls some device, such as a door, an alarm, a light, or a faucet.

A simple device controlled by a photoelectric current that you might investigate is a night light that goes on automatically when darkness falls. These are small-wattage lights that plug into an electric outlet in a hall-way, bedroom, or bathroom. You'll find a small area on the fixture on the side opposite the prongs of the plug that is light-sensitive. In daylight the light will not be on. What happens when you cover the light-sensitive area with your hand?

In a dark room the light will go on. You can turn it off by shining a light on it. Will the light go off if you shine red light on it? Will it go off if you shine infrared light on it? What does this tell you about the wavelength of the light needed to activate this photocell?

PHOTOELECTRICITY AND THE PARTICLE MODEL OF LIGHT • The reason scientists began to question the wave model is related to the experiment you performed with light and an electroscope. You probably noticed that if the electroscope carried a negative charge, it began to discharge the moment you shined the ultraviolet light on it. There was no delay. When scientists first tried to explain the photoelectric effect, they calculated the amount of energy delivered to the charged atoms in the photoelectric surface by light. They were surprised to find that their calculations showed that some time would be required before enough energy would accumulate to move the charges. In fact, in dim light it would be minutes or hours before they would expect to see any discharge. Yet the photoelectric effect was immediate. As soon as ultraviolet light fell on the charged metallic surface, whether on an electroscope or in an evacuated tube, it began to discharge.

In addition, the wave model predicted that after a certain delay there would be a sudden release of charge resulting in a current surge. During this interval, the many identically charged atoms would absorb energy from the passing wave fronts. Since the energy was believed to be spread evenly over the wave, many atoms would acquire the energy needed for discharge at about the same time. In fact, there was no delay and no surge of charge. The current was immediate and reasonably steady, even in dim light.

Furthermore, for each metal there was a critical wavelength. If the light shining on a certain charged metal had a wavelength greater then the metal's critical wavelength, the metal would *not* discharge. For metals such as zinc and copper, this critical wavelength was in the ultraviolet range. For the more active metals such as sodium and lithium, the critical wavelength was in the visible light. According to the wave model it might take longer for a long wavelength to discharge a metal than a shorter wavelength, but it could not explain the existence of a critical wavelength. Clearly, something was wrong with the wave model of light.

In 1905, Albert Einstein suggested that light comes to us in the form of tiny bundles of energy called *photons* ("particles" of energy, if you will). He showed that the energy of the photons depended on the frequency of the light. Ultraviolet light, which has a short wavelength relative to visible light, has a relatively large frequency. According to Einstein, the energy of photons is proportional to the frequency of the light. Therefore, photons of ultraviolet light should carry more energy than photons of visible light, which have a longer wavelength and a lower frequency.

A certain amount of energy is required to remove charge from an atom. A variety of experiments showed that it takes more energy to remove negative charge (electrons) from, say, an atom of zinc than from an atom of sodium. Therefore, discharging the atoms of zinc requires the more energetic photons found in ultraviolet light, whereas the less energetic photons that make up visible light can remove electrons from sodium.

Since light energy comes in "bundles" that depend on the frequency of the light, an atom need not "sit around" for long periods of time absorbing small amounts of energy from a tiny segment of the wave fronts that pass through it. Instead, if by chance it is hit by a photon with sufficient energy, it can absorb the energy it needs to escape the atom from this single photon.

Einstein's photon model successfully explained the photoelectric effect and many other phenomena at the atomic level. It led scientists to the realization that neither a wave nor a particle (photon) model can explain all the properties of light; both have their limitations. Consequently, we use whichever one best describes the events being observed.

If your school has a photoelectric cell, good color filters or a mercury light source with a lens and prism, a meter that will measure the small currents produced, and a means of placing a retarding voltage on the cell, you might like to investigate the effect of light intensity and wavelength on the photoelectric current. By adjusting the prism, or by using filters of different colors, you can shine light of varying wavelength (color) on the photoelectric cell. By determining the retarding voltage that just stops the current, you can measure the energy of the electrons produced when these different wavelengths of light shine on the photoelectric surface.

How is the energy of the electrons related to the wavelength of the light that shines on the photoelectric surface?

Also you might want to increase or decrease the intensity of the light shining on the photoelectric surface by moving a small light bulb closer to or farther from the photoelectric cell. How is the photoelectric current related to the intensity of the light shining on the photoelectric surface?

EPILOGUE

The experiments you have done while using this book have led you to understand how light reflects, refracts, and diffracts. Along the way, you have learned that light can be polarized and that both the refraction and the diffraction of light can give rise to colors. These colors normally reside hidden in the mixture of colored lights that we refer to as ordinary white light.

You have seen the beautiful interference patterns that can arise when light diffracts, the spectra produced by prisms, and the new colors that appear when colored lights are mixed by addition or subtraction, and perhaps you have come to appreciate the beauty inherent in colored shadows.

You have learned also that two theories—a wave model and a particle model—were developed to explain the behavior of light. Scientists argued about the validity of these two models for centuries. However, Thomas Young's success in producing interference patterns, together with experiments proving that light travels faster in air than in water, convinced most nineteenth-century scientists that light was really wavelike.

As often happens in science, their complacency was shaken when it was found that a wave model could not explain the photoelectric effect discovered by Hertz in 1888. Only a model based on photons could explain this effect. With photons, light is viewed once more as having a particlelike nature. But photons are not regarded as miniature billiard balls. They are tiny bundles of energy that can produce interference effects just as waves can.

Experiments have shown again and again that light has the qualities that make us think of it as particles and the qualities that lead us to regard it as wavelike. It is neither, and yet it is both. Words cannot convey the true nature of light. Only through the language of mathematics can its true nature be expressed.

If you are interested in penetrating more deeply into the nature of light, you not only will want to bone up on your math but will want to prepare yourself for more advanced books and courses that will draw upon your knowledge of both mathematics and physics. Perhaps you will be able to contribute one day to a further understanding of the nature of light. Perhaps you will find that behind the apparent wave/particle duality is a heretofore undiscovered unity.

APPENDIX:
SCIENTIFIC SUPPLY
COMPANIES

Carolina Biological Supply Co.
2700 York Road
Burlington, NC 27215

Central Scientific Co. (CENCO)
11222 Melrose Avenue
Frankin Park, IL 60131

Connecticut Valley Biological
    Supply Co., Inc.
82 Valley Road
Southampton, Ma 01073

Delta Education
P.O. Box M
Nashua, NH 03061

Edmund Scientific Co.
101 East Gloucester Pike
Barrington, NJ 08007

Fisher Scientific Co.
4901 W. LeMoyne Street
Chicago, IL 60651

Frey Scientific Co.
905 Hickory Lane
Mansfield, OH 44905

McKilligan Supply Corp.
435 Main Street
Johnson City, NY 13790

Nasco Science
901 Janesville Road
Fort Atkinson, WI 53538

Nasco West Inc.
P.O. Box 3837
Modesto, CA 95352

Schoolmasters Science
P.O. Box 1941
Ann Arbor, MI 48106

Science Kit & Boreal Laboratories
777 East Park Drive
Tonawanda, NY 14150–6782
                    or
P.O. Box 2726
Santa Fe Springs, CA 90670–4490

Wards Natural Science
    Establishment, Inc.
5100 West Henrietta Road
P.O. Box 92912
Rochester, NY 14692

FOR FURTHER READING

Asimov, Isaac. *How Did We Find Out About the Speed of Light?* New York: Walker, 1986.

Graf, Calvin R. *Exploring Light, Radio, and Sound: With Projects*. Blue Ridge Summit, Pa.: TAB books, 1985.

Haber-Schaim Uri, John Dodge, and James Walter. *PSSC Physics*. Lexington, Mass.: D. C. Heath, 1986.

Hill, Julie, and Julian Hill. *Looking at Light and Color*. N. Pomfret, Vt.: David and Charles, 1986.

Hecht, Jeff. *Optics: Light for a New Age*. New York: Macmillan, 1987.

Heuer, Kenneth. *Rainbows, Halos, and Other Wonders: Light and Color in the Atmosphere*. New York: Dodd, Mead, 1978.

Holton, Gerald, James S. Rutherford, and Fletcher G. Watson, Directors of Harvard Project Physics. *Project Physics*. Forth Worth, Tex.: Holt, Rinehart, and Winston, 1975.

_____. *The Project Physics Course Handbook*. Fort Worth, Tex.: Holt, Rinehart, and Winston, 1975.

Jaffe, Bernard. *Michelson and the Speed of Light*. Westport, Conn.: Greenwood, 1979.

Levin, Edith. *The Penetrating Beam: Reflections on Light*. New York: Rosen Group, 1979.

Light and its Uses: Making and Using Lasers, Holograms, Interferometers & Instruments of Dispersion—Readings from Scientific American, intro. by Jearl Walker. San Francisco: W.H. Freeman, 1980.

Minnaert, M. *The Nature of Light & Color in the Open Air*. New York: Dover, 1954.

Riley, Peter. *Light and Sound*. N. Pomfret, Vt.: David and Charles, 1986.

Shull, Jim. *The Hole Thing*. Dobbs Ferry, N.Y.: Morgan and Morgan, 1975.

INDEX

Grazing angle, 41–42

Haidinger's brush, 113–114
Hertz, Heinrich, 118, 129
Horizon, 34
Horizontal axis, 27
Huygens, Christian, 67

Images, multi, 26–27
Incident ray, 17, 18, 22
Independent variable, 27
Induction, 122
Interference patterns, 79,
    85, *87, 88, 89, 91, 93,
    96, 98, 99, 101*
        using diffraction
            grating, 102–103
Iris (eye), 54–55

Lasers, 35
Law of reflection, *16,* 22
Lens, magic, experiment,
    35–*36*
Light
    bending, 28–45
    characteristics of, 129
    defining ray of, 30–32
    diffraction of, 85–86
    interference of, 97–
        102
    measuring angles of,
        rays, *19*
    particle model of, 62–
        66
    polarized, 109–110
    predicting paths of, 30
    properties of, 62
    ray, 14, *23, 31*

reflection, 13–27
refraction, 30
spread of, 62
straight paths of, 13–
    14
theories of, 61–62
twinkling, 34–35
white, 30
Longitudinal waves, 108

Magenta, 42
Maxima, 90, 92, *99,* 100
Mirror image, 18–*20*
    characteristics of, 21
Mirrors
    angle experiments
        with, 23–27, *26*
    and mixed light, 43
Mixing colored light, *41*

Newton, Isaac, 9
Nodal lines, 85, 88, 90, 92,
    94, *99,* 100
Nodes, 90
Normal, a, 17, 32, 65

Optical illusion, *24*

Parallax, 20–21
Particle model of light, 62–
    66
    analogy, *63, 65*
    and photoelectricity,
        124–127
    problems with, 66–67
    and reflection, 63
    and refraction, 64–66

139

ABOUT
THE AUTHOR

Robert Gardner taught biology, chemistry, physics, and physical science at Salisbury School in Salisbury, Connecticut, for more than thirty years prior to his retirement. Mr. Gardner's books on science for children and young adults have won numerous awards and citations. His *Experimenting with Illusions* was named by *Science Books and Films* to its Best Children's Science Book List for 1990. Robert Gardner's other recent books for Franklin Watts include *Ideas for Science Projects, More Ideas for Science Projects, Famous Experiments You Can Do*, and *Experimenting with Inventions*. He now lives on Cape Cod with his wife, Natalie.